DETOUR NEBRASKA

DETOUR NEBRASKA

HISTORIC DESTINATIONS & NATURAL WONDERS

GRETCHEN M. GARRISON

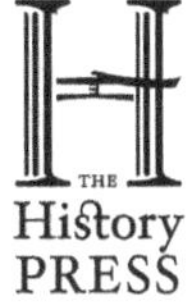

Published by The History Press
Charleston, SC
www.historypress.net

All images are courtesy of the author unless otherwise noted.

First published 2017

Manufactured in the United States

ISBN 9781625858818

Library of Congress Control Number: 2017945009

Notice: The information in this book is true and complete to the best of our knowledge. It is offered without guarantee on the part of the author or The History Press. The author and The History Press disclaim all liability in connection with the use of this book.

CONTENTS

ACKNOWLEDGEMENTS

Thank you to those of you in my personal community who encouraged and supported me through this writing process, including the Upper Room, my CENTER co-op, Girlie Gourmands, #LNK Blog Love and too many others to mention.

Love to our Michels, Gustafson, Garrison and Dolezal families!

Thank you Amie, Chad, Abigail, Katie, Annie, Suzy, Becky, Sarah and Dennis, Kim, Tonya and especially Brenna for your assistance with photo selection, book formatting and travel. Thank you to Tim and Lisa of the Walking Tourists for your support and for letting me use three of your wonderful photographs.

Thank you to my supportive husband, Papa and Grandma, Grammi and Poppa along with Aunt She-She for taking on the kids so I could write. I especially would like to thank my parents for taking us places growing up. To them, my siblings and their families: thanks for being such a sweet part of my journey!

To my Kyle, Gabriel, Zechariah, Kaylee and Isaac—you are the best part of my odyssey through Nebraska. Love you!

Deepest gratitude to the Author of my life who whispered on my heart one June morning that I should write about Nebraska. Without your eternal presence, none of this would have been possible.

INTRODUCTION

Purposefully exploring Nebraska became my mission in the summer of 2013. Having been a mommy blogger, I felt nudged to change directions. As our homeschool history topic for that year was Nebraska, I decided to start a new blog, *Odyssey through Nebraska*. My tagline: the places and people of Nebraska, both past and present. Having already planned some Nebraska travel, our destinations became more deliberate.

As we traveled around, this focus led to more than I expected about the unofficial Good Life State. Connecting to the history in a firsthand way brought the stories of my state to life. Even the Nebraska detours have been an adventure.

Lessons Learned along the Way

First of all, so many people are proud (and rightfully so!) of their museums and attractions. Talking to a person is often more informative than reading the placard signs. Asking questions is the best way to learn.

Second, Nebraska tends to be a seasonal state. Many locations mentioned in this book are only open late spring through early fall. Nebraska's two time zones can also affect travel plans. Some places are laid-back about their hours, especially in the smaller communities. At times, we traveled to places that ended up being randomly closed. Calling first is recommended.

Third, parts of Nebraska are rather remote. Because of this fact, cellphone coverage can be limited. Traveling with an actual map is recommended. Bring along water, and fill up the gas tank. In more isolated areas, many miles pass between towns.

LOCATIONS ORGANIZATION

This book has divided Nebraska into seven regions. To visit all featured locations found in one region could take up to a week. Yes, one could spend several weeks touring Nebraska and not come close to visiting everywhere. Attempts were made to put places in a logical order. Regional travel is only one way to travel around the state. Look at a Nebraska map to plot out your best routes. Thanks to Nebraska Tourism for letting me use the area designations found in one of its tourism magazines. Most of all, thank you for joining me as we travel to Nebraska destinations!

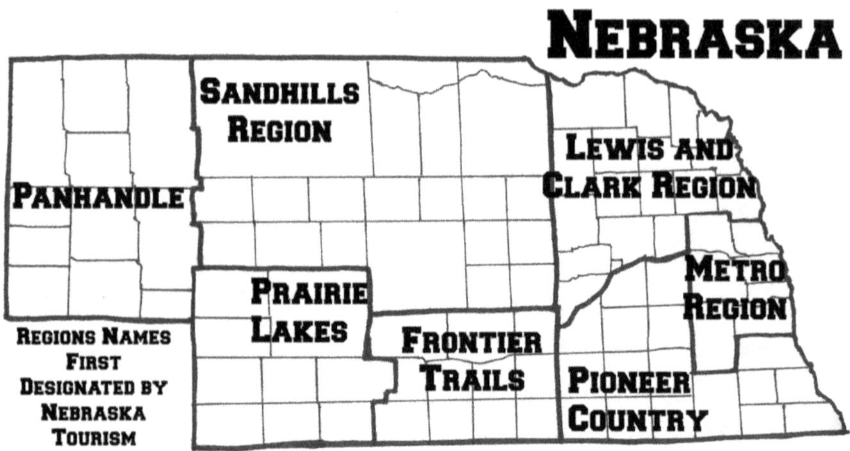

This Nebraska map designates the regions used in this book.

1
METRO REGION

Although this part of Nebraska may seem urban now, this region was once a vast, unsettled plain. Early settlers were visionaries.

Fort Atkinson State Historical Park, Just Outside of Fort Calhoun

Nebraska's first military post was Camp Catonement. Missouri River flooding necessitated relocation to the top of the original Council Bluff. Here Lewis and Clark first met with area Native Americans during their Louisiana Purchase Expedition. The site became Fort Atkinson in 1820.

Protecting fur trade interests and keeping the peace was the fort's mission. About 1,200 soldiers were at this official garrison. At the time, that was one-quarter of the U.S. Army. Here Nebraska's first school and library opened. A gristmill, sawmill and brickyard were built. Less than a decade had passed before this site was deemed unnecessary. Once the army realigned south, soldiers and their families moved on.

For over a century, this site existed as farmland. Besides a small monument, nothing hinted at the former history. In the 1950s, archaeologists uncovered building remains and countless artifacts. Soon after, the Fort Atkinson Foundation began reconstructing some former fort buildings.

Travelers can visit the rebuilt wooden fort. During summers, the visitor's center presents fort life in detail. Periodic living history weekends provide the best times to visit. Volunteers reenact 1820s fort life in a variety of ways. Watching the infantry march in formation or the coopers creating barrels brings history to life. Kids complete scavenger hunts for rock candy rewards. With a Nebraska State Park permit and small entrance fee, guests can experience early Nebraska.

BELLEVUE, NEBRASKA'S FIRST OFFICIAL SETTLEMENT

In 1822, the Missouri Fur Company built a trading post at what is now Bellevue. In 1828, the American Fur Company took over. Lucien Fontenelle, who had once overseen the upriver Fort Lisa, became the operator. Once trading ceased, the U.S. government started the Missouri River Indian Agency. At one time, missionaries Moses and Eliza Merrill also had a mission here before moving to a nearby permanent location. Colonel Peter Sarpy started a ferry system near the river. All of these early settlers made their mark on this area.

Today, the original trading posts are gone, but some historic buildings are still in town. On Hancock Street is a log cabin that dates to 1835. Settlers built the Main Street Fontenelle Bank in 1856. As the state's oldest bank, it could both issue and circulate money in the Nebraska Territory. That same year, Franklin Street Old Presbyterian Church was established. Original stained-glass windows and oak pews are still intact.

Bellevue almost became Nebraska's capital. The first territorial governor, Francis Burt, planned on settling there. While traveling west to start governing Nebraska, he fell ill and did not live long enough to make that happen. Omaha became the territorial capital instead.

FONTENELLE FOREST

Setting aside 1,500 acres of forestland in an urban area requires foresight. Over a century ago, the Fontenelle Forest Association began to protect this unique ecosystem. The forest has become more accessible to visitors. Preserving this National Natural Landmark is still important.

Part of the loess hills region, this area's thick soil is fertile ground. Trees thrive and provide numerous shady exploring opportunities. Using provided trail information, hikers can explore at their own ability levels. The constructed boardwalk is an easy trail. For those unafraid of mud, paths wind through floodplain areas.

One trail is a literal walk through history. Many Indian tribes lived, traveled and traded at this site. Former earth lodges' indentations are evident. Remains mark the Office of Indian Affairs' temporary post. Pilcher's Post, later Fontenelle's trading post site, is noted with a memorial marker. This post and Peter Sarpy's ferry landing spot hint at Omaha's beginnings. Pioneers traveled through the section known now as the Mormon Hollow Trail. The trails of the former Child's Logging Mill are now used by hikers. Throughout the southern upland history trail, fifteen specific sites illuminate the past.

Encouraging family exploration is one of Fontenelle Forest's primary goals. With nine interactive stations, the designed Acorn Acres is a forest playground. Educational opportunities often involve wildlife. Critter encounters provide children with the opportunity to observe animals up close. Planned programs and camps gear learning toward specific age groups.

Adults will also enjoy visiting this forest. Birding enthusiasts can watch for 246 bird species known to fly through these trees. The insect club searches for the littlest creatures. Even a Frogwatch USA group exists to monitor the amphibian population. The photo club captures this breathtaking place on film.

Nearby, Neale Woods provides six hundred more acres of urban paradise managed by Fontenelle Forest. Hikers will enjoy this area. On site, stargazers can enjoy Millard Observatory, Omaha's largest.

Besides maintaining these acres, these land stewards complete other missions. They are restoring the declining oak woodlands. The growing deer population is managed. Erosion control protocols protect the threatened marshes, and scheduled controlled burns restore nature's balance. Eradicating invasive species helps desired plants to grow. In addition to trained staff, this location relies on volunteers. To continue forest conservation, admission is charged at both locations.

OMAHA

As territorial capital, Omaha should have been thriving. But between river traffic and the railroad, the town was not always the best place to be. *A Dirty Wicked Town: Tales of Nineteenth Century Omaha* by David Bristow reveals much about Omaha's shady beginnings. When deciding on the location of the Nebraska state capitol, everyone wanted a new location—other than the Omaha residents, of course.

From its founding in 1868, Fort Omaha changed purposes multiple times. When the fort was headquarters for the Department of the Platte, soldiers passed out supplies to the army. These men were protecting territory that stretched to Montana. In 1879, the fort held the trial of Standing Bear, which legally proved that Native Americans were people.

The next season involved balloons. For eight years, the Signal Corps School operated here, later known as Fort Omaha Balloon School. Balloon operators trained at Fort Omaha. By floating above battlegrounds, these balloons were considered the eyes of the army.

During World War II, the fort held supplies and worked Italian prisoners of war. In 1947, the army gave the fort to the navy for its Naval and Marine Corps reserve center. From 1951 to 1974, the fort was designated the U.S. Naval Personnel Center. Then military use stopped.

Now the Metropolitan Community College uses most buildings. The Douglas County Historical Society utilizes General Crook's former home as its headquarters and as an early fort life museum.

FLORENCE

Now part of Omaha, Florence was once its own thriving community. From 1846 to 1848, Mormons heading west wintered here. Today, Mormon Trail Center Tours tell of these pioneers who traveled toward a better life. Nearby is the Florence Mill. First the mill fed the pioneers, and then it supported the new town of Florence. Although this structure is being remodeled, some original hand-hewn beams and wooden pegs remain. On the walls are historic photos and artifacts from the pioneer era. This location is now also the ArtLoft Gallery. During the summer, artistic events take place.

Durham Museum

The story of the Durham Museum starts with the railroad. Union Pacific's headquarters were in Omaha, and the current railroad station did not reflect that status. Art deco architect Gilbert Stanley Underwood designed a masterpiece. Soon Union Station became one of the busiest stations in the country. With the mid- to late century decline of passenger railways, the station closed its doors, but the railroad donated the beautiful building to Omaha.

In 1975, the Western Heritage Museum opened, featuring small regional exhibits. Twenty years later, Union Station underwent renovations, and operations began on a larger scale. Renamed Durham Western Heritage Museum, the new Smithsonian affiliate started educational programming. Growth continues.

Besides the beautiful architectural elements, the station's former purpose is evident. Guests can order drinks from the 1931 soda fountain. In the Great Hall are Omaha sculptor John Lajba's six groups of passenger

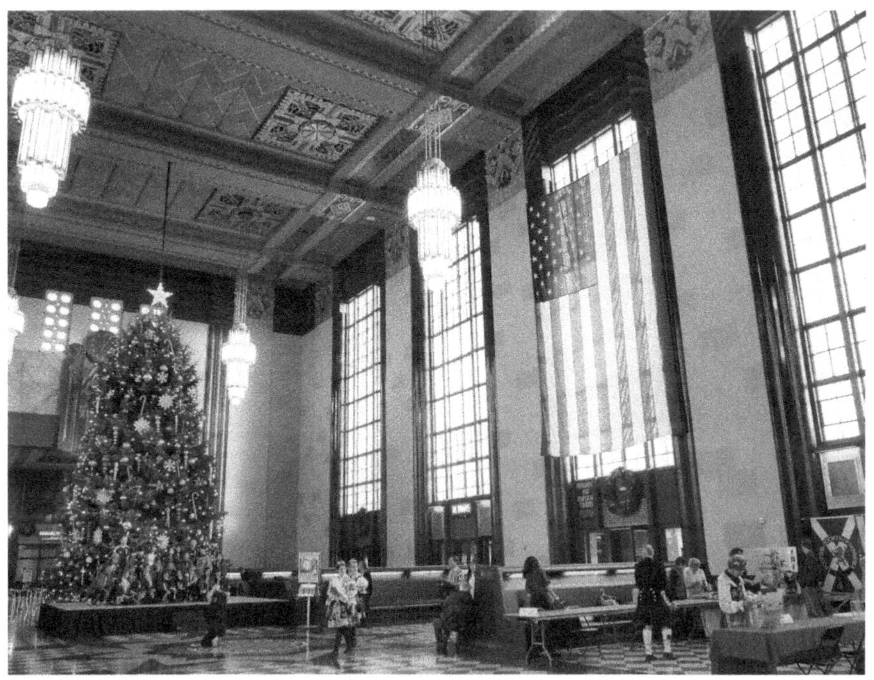

The Durham Museum in Omaha has an ethnic holiday festival each December.

statues. They authenticate the station's former purpose. Downstairs, guests can see a steam engine and board train cars, including a Pullman sleeper, a lounge car and a caboose.

Permanent exhibits tell the story of Omaha's history from the Buffet Grocery Store to the 1940s streetcar. From an earth lodge to the blue-collar worker's cottage and a 1950s dream home prototype, structures show early Omaha housing. In the Trans-Mississippi Exposition Gallery, the White City has been rebuilt in miniature. This 1898 world's fair brought people to town. Area real estate agent Byron Reed collected documents and coins, including a rare 1804 dollar. Upon Reed's death in 1891, his collection was donated to the City of Omaha and is cared for by the museum.

Throughout the year, temporary exhibits fill one large gallery. Past displays have included Lost Egypt, Katharine Hepburn, Buffalo Bill's Wild West Show and the Kennedy Photograph Collection. Educational programming and other opportunities expand on the themes.

Joslyn Castle

In the early Omaha community, few were more important than George and Sarah Joslyn. When they built their hilltop home on Omaha's edge, their plans reflected their stature. Architect John McDonald designed a Scottish baronial castle for the Joslyns in 1903. Less than one year later, the couple moved into their four-story, thirty-five-room home.

From the gold drawing room to the expansive ballroom, guests were welcomed into grandeur. Later, a music room was added. At one time, bowling and poker happened downstairs. The home had many entertaining purposes.

Just as breathtaking was their landscaping. From the indoor conservatory to an onsite greenhouse, beautiful flowers abounded. The gardeners cultivated rare and exotic plants from all over the globe. Today, the still expansive grounds are a part of the Nebraska Statewide Arboretum.

Although her husband died in 1916, Sarah remained at the castle until her 1940 death. For forty-five years, the Omaha Public Schools headquartered at the castle. Then the state took over. Joslyn Trust managed the castle and would later purchase the building and grounds.

Today, tours highlighting the house take place certain Sunday afternoons. During December, the home is decorated for Christmas. Unique "Joslyn

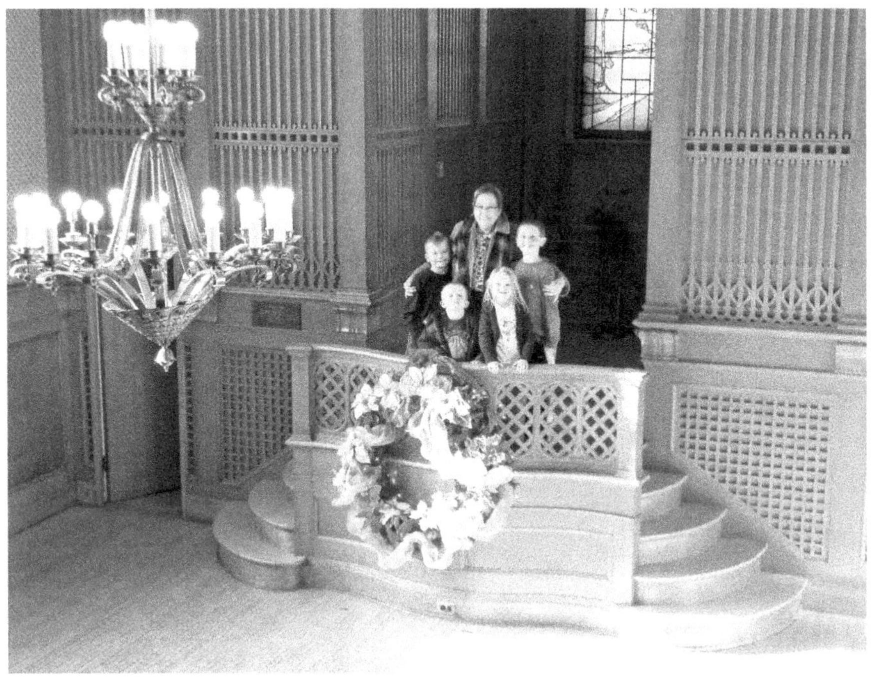

The music room at Joslyn Castle is still used for events today.

Unlocked" tours provide a more in-depth glimpse into all levels of the home. Special events, such as literary festivals and theater productions, happen throughout the year. Joslyn Castle may be rented out for weddings, receptions and gatherings.

Joslyn Art Museum

After her husband George's death, Sarah Joslyn wanted to honor his memory and highlight their mutual love of music and art. Opening a concert hall surrounded with galleries would certainly encourage art appreciation. In late 1931, the beautiful art deco Joslyn Memorial opened. Imported stone and marble variations transformed the building into a masterpiece of its own. In 1994, the Walter and Suzanne Scott Pavilion expanded this museum. A glass atrium connects the two buildings. Flanking both ends are two expansive sculptures by glass artist Dale Chihuly.

Inside, the museum's permanent collection is extensive. From classical artists like Degas to western artists like George Catlin, pieces vary in style and composition. Ancient, European, American, American Indian, American West, Asian, Latin American and contemporary art are all at home here. Several rotating themed exhibitions are featured in the pavilion. Although the museum is free, some temporary exhibits have a ticket charge.

Educating the public about art is another priority at the Joslyn. Interactive opportunities abound for students. All educational sectors are represented: preschool, public, private and homeschool. Students of all ages can take drawing, painting and even photography classes. Art schools and art camps add another level of learning. Training for teachers and mentorships round out this educational component.

Connecting visitors of all ages to art is the goal in the newer Art Works room. Designed for smaller groups to interact with the museum, this cozy room defines creativity. From the spectrum sculpture to the animation station, children can make masterpieces. One center is designated for art projects that relate directly to the current temporary exhibition found upstairs. Children love being able to paint on a computer and film stop-motion clips.

Outside, the sculpture garden allows visitors to walk and enjoy art; the statues dotting the grounds invite exploration. The upfront Peter Kiewit Foundation Sculpture Garden is more formal. To the north of the building, the Discovery Garden displays creativity in the finest sense. Paths connecting the art pieces encourage children to run along and experience artwork. One cannot help but think that Sarah Joslyn would be pleased with how her husband's memorial has continued to evolve.

KANEKO

Growing up in Japan may have set Jun Kaneko up to be an internationally known artist. His artwork is definitely bigger than life. Since 1986, Kaneko has worked out of Omaha. Twelve years later, Kaneko and his wife, Ree, started a nonprofit to encourage others to engage creatively.

Located in Old Market warehouses, Kaneko is coined as "an open space for your mind." Collaborating Kaneko team members coordinate different themes that encourage interaction. Exhibits rotate about every quarter. Each collection looks at art and often science in unexpected ways. Programs, camps and outreach events compel patrons to take their imaginations to a new level.

Gerald R. Ford Conservation Center

On July 4, 1913, Leslie King Jr. was born in Omaha. While the King name is unfamiliar, Gerald Ford's name is not. Due to his mother's divorce and remarriage, both Ford's original name and time in Omaha were short. Fire destroyed that first home, so tours are not possible. However, gardens planted at the site do welcome guests.

The Gerald R. Ford Conservation Center, a division of the Nebraska State Historical Society, was built on the adjacent property. A display honors our nation's thirty-eighth president. The rest of this location is devoted to conservation of art and historic artifacts. Preserving objects, paintings and paper for museums and private individuals is the primary purpose of this location.

Lauritzen Gardens and the Omaha Henry Doorly Zoo

"Escape to an urban oasis." This tagline of the Lauritzen Gardens captures the heart of its location. While enjoying this lush setting, visitors might forget that they are near downtown Omaha.

The garden exemplifies visionary efforts to provide a serene setting for the study, preservation and enjoyment of nature. In 1982, a group of volunteers began a grass-roots effort to build a botanical garden in Omaha. A bluff with wooded terrain was selected as the perfect location. After tireless planning and fundraising efforts, Lauritzen Gardens first opened in 1995. The first areas open for visitors were a rose and shade garden. Herbs were also growing. Guests could walk along a flowering path.

Over the next two decades, the garden expanded. Today, Lauritzen Gardens encompasses one hundred acres and more than twenty themed displays. At the visitor and education center, guests can enjoy indoor horticultural displays year round. The recently constructed Majorie K. Daugherty Conservatory expanded the indoor plant offerings.

The impressive model railroad garden is open outdoors from May to October. Constructed from natural materials, miniature Omaha buildings provide the perfect backdrop for G-scale trains. Complete with tunnels and wooden bridges, the seven lines of track delight visitors. During the holiday season, the trains come indoors. Looking for trains darting among the poinsettia plants keeps observers busy for hours.

Throughout the year, Lauritzen Gardens has special events, educational programs and art exhibits. Certain flowers, such as the orchid and chrysanthemum, are shown annually. Camps bring life to children's summers. An extra fee, beyond regular admission, is charged for many of these additional events.

Just down the street is the Henry Doorly Zoo and Aquarium. Considered a world-class zoological center, the multiple animal habitat zones exude excellence. Walking under the sea and strolling through the rainforest are simply starting points. Animal conservation and education are also cornerstones. Spend the day here for an unforgettable experience.

BOYS TOWN AND FATHER FLANAGAN

A true religious training for children is most essential if we are expected to develop them into good men and good women—worthy citizens of our great country.
—Father Flanagan

Growing up in Ireland, Father Flanagan knew harsh conditions. After early immigration to the United States, he later trained for the priesthood. In 1912, Flanagan started his Nebraska service. Over time, his concern grew for homeless and orphaned boys. Right before Christmas 1917, he and five boys moved into the first Father Flanagan's Boys Home. As their needs grew, so did Flanagan's mission. In 1921, the move to Overlook Farm meant more space to make an impact. Through the years, hundreds of boys and later girls would find needed helpful support at what became Boys Town.

Flanagan also traveled to speak out in support of children and families. Parental responsibility was encouraged. The welfare of children and prison reform were two important topics. Father Flanagan had a heart for people.

Today, Boys Town is still making an impact in Omaha. Boys and girls come to find hope. While helping the next generation, Boys Town remembers its past. Father Flanagan's former home is now a museum. At the Hall of History museum, visitors learn more about the organization's worldwide outreach and effect. Various artifacts and sound clips bring Boys Town's mission to life.

Two Rivers State Recreation Area Near Venice

For less than $100 per night, a rare camping experience awaits. Ten former Union Pacific cabooses have been reoutfitted as cabins. Each one sleeps six and contains both bathroom and kitchen. Plan ahead, because bedding and towels are not provided.

Strategic Air Command and Aerospace Museum Near Ashland

If we maintain our faith in God, love of freedom and superior global air power, the future looks good.
—General Curtis LeMay

As the first commander-in-chief of the Strategic Air Command (SAC), from 1949 to 1957, General Curtis LeMay had a tough job. This "Father of Sac" was responsible for multiple missions and nuclear bomber planes. Due to his high training standards and demanding evaluations, LeMay turned SAC into a professional, effective nuclear-capable military force. Under his leadership, SAC added both national and international Air Force bases. SAC was operated out of Offutt Air Force Base. During his command, the number of personnel and tactical aircraft increased dramatically.

General LeMay proposed displaying the airplanes once used to keep the peace. At first, exhibits were displayed at the Bellevue base. In 1998, the museum moved aircraft and artifacts to a new 330,000-square-foot facility halfway between Lincoln and Omaha.

This accessible museum's two end hangars are filled with various aircraft from World War II and the Cold War. From the RF-4C "Phantom II" to the B-17G Flying Fortress, all thirty-plus planes appear to be ready for takeoff at any moment. Signs tell about each aircraft. Rockets, missiles and spacecraft are also on hand. Standing close to these giant airplanes is breathtaking.

After years of eroding outdoors, worn-out aircraft undergo restoration. Along with volunteers, the small staff works in the Durham Restoration Hangar. About ten thousand man hours are needed to fix up one of these giant jets. Restoration is limited to fixing up the planes for display purposes. Too much time, money and effort is required to make these venerable aircraft flight-worthy.

Besides the aircraft and aerospace aspect, this museum encourages education. Rotating exhibits feature themes that revolve around the subjects of math and science. In the permanent children's learning gallery, interactive centers inspire kids to learn about scientific principles. Field trips and robotics instruction along with space and aviation camps are offered. Throughout the year, private and public events take place at the museum. This nonprofit museum charges admission to continue its mission. When visiting, allow several hours to fully enjoy the experience.

Lee G. Simmons Conservation Park and Wildlife Safari

Just off the interstate, visitors can experience a Nebraska-style safari. This drive-through park features North American animals in their natural habitats. As the animals roam freely, safety precautions are important. All visitors must be inside closed vehicles, and no animal feeding is allowed.

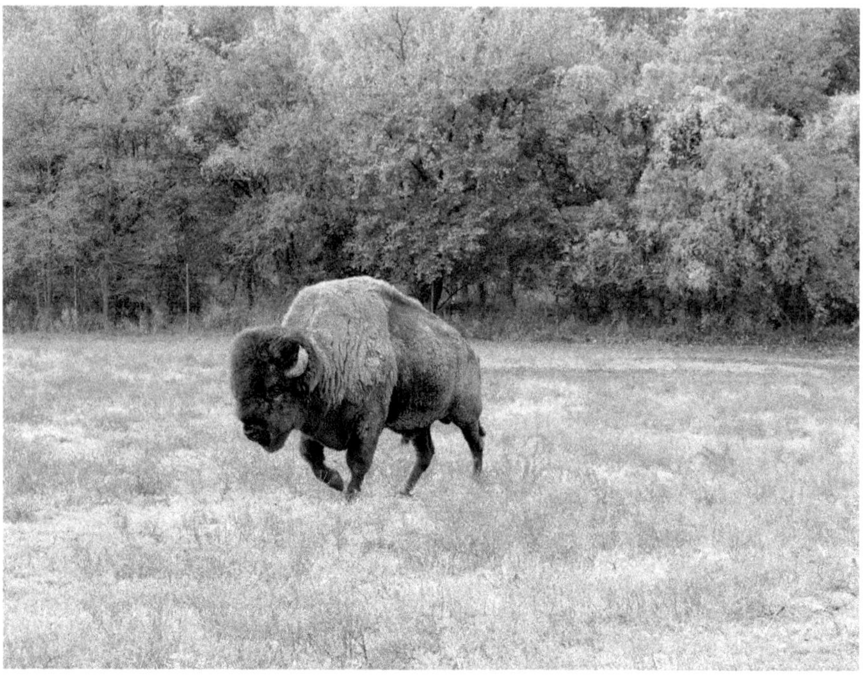

Drive through the Lee G. Simmons Conservation Park and Wildlife Safari to see the bison in a native setting.

From the car, visitors can see the elk, eagle, deer, buffalo and water bird habitats. At one point, guests can walk to a few places. A farmyard area lets kids feed the goats. A short hike is required to see the bears and wolves.

Metro State Parks and Recreation Areas Plus Springfield Drug

Within a small area are three fantastic state parks. At the site of the state's first 1882 fish hatchery is a fishing management museum, Schramm State Recreational Area. Its Ak-Sar-Ben Aquarium displays fifty Nebraska fish, including a giant catfish. The nearby Platte River State Park is known for its tall observatory tower overlooking the river.

Mahoney State Park is the largest of the metro state parks. During summer, visitors can water slide into the swimming pool or play miniature golf. The indoor activity center includes a giant play structure. An attached ice-skating rink provides winter fun. Horseback riding is possible, too. With only the requirement of a Nebraska state park permit, all three locations provide ample hiking and camping opportunities.

After stopping at these parks, visit the nearby Historic Springfield Drug. Displays show off historic pharmaceuticals. At the old-fashioned soda fountain, treats are available along with a fun photo opportunity. When *The Simpsons Movie* cartoon came out, producers contacted towns named Springfield across the country. For a bit of promotion, participating sites would receive commemorative displays. Now life-size Simpson sculptures fill up half a wooden bench. Visitors can now literally picture themselves with Homer, Marge, Bart, Lisa and Maggie.

Weeping Water Valley Historical Society Museum Complex

In Weeping Water, three historic buildings tell about early town life. Dr. Fate's medical office and Heritage House are two of them. Using homeopathic remedies, this doctor's practice was progressive. Besides original equipment, some treatments line medical dispenser shelves. At the former church parsonage, Fate family members called Heritage House their home. Today, visitors can tour the home and see many original furnishings. Highlighted in the Kunkel building are area citizens and geological history. The Memory Lane Museum catalogues town business history.

BESS STREETER ALDRICH HOUSE AND MUSEUM IN ELMWOOD

A small town is a good place for a writer to live. Not only is he close to the people and so close to life in the raw, but also it keeps him humble.
—from Bess Streeter Aldrich's article "Why I Live in a Small Town," Ladies' Home Journal, *1933*

Bess Streeter Aldrich won her first prizes for writing as a teenager. As an Iowa State Normal student and then a teacher, telling stories was less of a priority. When Aldrich was a new mom, she and her husband, Charles, relocated to Elmwood, Nebraska. There they operated a bank along with her sister and brother-in-law. Their widowed mother moved to town as well. Elmwood became home and the setting for many a story Aldrich told.

In 1911, Aldrich entered a *Ladies' Home Journal* fiction contest. Her top-six finish convinced her to find more writing time. In tribute to her grandmothers, she initially used a pseudonym, Margaret Dean Stephens. For the next decade, Aldrich wrote in snatches. Often dishwater covered her manuscript drafts. Her persistence paid off. In 1924, *Mother Mason*, a compilation of short stories, became her first published book.

Just before her full-length novel *Rim of the Prairie* came into print, tragedy struck the family. Charles Aldrich died suddenly. As a new widow, Bess needed to support her four children with her words. She rose to the challenge and used her writing to send all four to college.

Magazine readers loved her short stories. In all, Aldrich wrote over one hundred articles and made some available in collections. With a Midwest backdrop, many of her stories and novels told of pioneer settlers and small-town living. Over time, Aldrich wrote nine novels and a novella. Her most famous book, *A Lantern in Her Hand*, is one of my personal favorites.

During her later years, Aldrich moved to Lincoln to live closer to her daughter. The time had come for her to enjoy her family, and she completed little writing. She died in 1954 at the age of seventy-three.

Today, two Elmwood buildings allow visitors to learn more about Aldrich. Stepping inside the the Elms, her family home, takes visitors back several decades. In the sunny corner of the study, Bess's writing desk seems ready to tell more tales. The dining table is still set for mealtime, and many original family pieces are on display.

Blocks away is the Bess Streeter Aldrich Museum. An original manuscript and handwritten letters show Aldrich's script. As her book *Miss Bishop* was made into a movie, souvenirs from the set of *Cheers for Miss Bishop* are exhibited. Even Flossie, Bess's favorite childhood doll, is on display. The sites are open limited hours year round, and the price of admission covers both locations.

LINCOLN

When Nebraska became a state on March 1, 1867, Lincoln became the capital city. This move did not come without considerable effort. As territorial capital, Omaha did not want to lose its status. These Omaha leaders insisted that if the capital did move to the south of the Platte River, the new capital must be called Lincoln. While naming the capital after the most recent president seemed honorable, they had ulterior motives. Many southern Nebraskans were pro–Civil War and not big fans of the sixteenth president. But to their surprise, the name change was agreed upon, so the move was on.

The Capital Commission of Governor Butler, State Auditor Gillispie and Secretary of State Kennard would decide the location. Several communities were in the running for capital status but were gradually removed. Because of its river location, biting mosquitoes eliminated Ashland. The Town of Yankee Hill decided to improve its chances with a town social. After saving up ice and sugar, the ladies of the town made ice cream. Since this was possibly the first time the sweet treat had been served in Nebraska, this was momentous. However, the plan backfired, as the committee determined the dessert would seem like a bribe. Due to the proximity of salt flats, Lancaster was the final selection. On February 25, 1868, Lancaster became Lincoln. Right away, the commissioners set out to build homes for themselves. To encourage people to relocate, the new town of Lincoln needed to feel like an actual settlement.

Downtown Lincoln Houses

Only one of these first homes still stands today. The Thomas P. Kennard House from that original Lincoln plat is still downtown. Restored to its 1870s beginnings, the Victorian style influenced the home's decor. Each December, the home is decked out in old-fashioned fun for the holidays. On the Sunday of the Nebraska Capitol tree-lighting ceremony, this is one of three homes open for the holidays.

Next door, the Ferguson House was once home to one of Lincoln's founding families. Although now used as a business, the architectural history is still evident. Taking a tour is possible by appointment, but guides provide longer tours on the holiday open-house day.

Down the street is the Nebraska Governor's Residence. All year, this home is open for tours on Thursday afternoons. Throughout the home are decorative touches that symbolize Nebraska, such as cornstalks and sandhill cranes. The dining room features a Lewis and Clark discovery mural. Down the hall, portraits of former governors line the hall. In the basement is the prized collection of First Lady dolls wearing reproduction inaugural ball dresses. The state's one First Gentleman is in the mix. During December, a twelve-foot tree greets guests in the foyer. Purposeful holiday touches are found throughout the residence. This home is also open for special tours the day of the capitol tree-lighting ceremony.

THE NEBRASKA CAPITOL

The Designers

The first state capitol lasted about a decade, as inferior materials and construction resulted in rapid deterioration. The second building was not much better. Despite seven years of building, this structure remained unstable. Talk of replacement began before the building was even thirty years old.

A decade of discussion took place before any action happened. This time, officials were determined to plan a building that would last. Finding an architect with structurally sound ideas was the mission. Officials held a competition, and out of many nationwide firms, New York architect Bertram Goodhue was the winner.

Reflecting Nebraska history throughout the building was crucial. Because of the project's immensity, construction took a decade. To help achieve his architectural plans, Goodhue developed a strong team.

Hildreth Meière was the chosen mural artisan, but she made few trips to Nebraska. Instead, workers installed the murals sent from her New York studio designs. In 1928, Meière won the Gold Medal in Mural Painting from the Architectural League of New York. She considered the Nebraska Capitol her finest work.

Not all capitol murals were created by Meière, but she was a part of the selection committee for murals added in 1956. In honor of Nebraska's 1967 centennial, additional framed murals were completed by others.

Sculptor Lee Lawrie shaped the outside of the capitol, and his sculptures contribute to the building's style. The nineteen-foot-tall bronze *Sower* can be seen for miles.

An unexpected team member was Hartley Burr Alexander. As a University of Nebraska philosophy professor, he also studied Native American cultures. His expertise added authenticity to the designs and kept them true to Nebraska. Alexander determined what quotes should line certain walls.

Around the Nebraska Capitol

Strolling around the exterior walkway of the Nebraska Capitol is an education. To start, the names of all ninety-three Nebraska counties are etched in stone. This building also provides a visual lesson in government and democracy. The twenty-one dimensional sculptures located above the promenade capture historic civic moments. Reliefs represent both ancient and modern law. The Nebraska Capitol brochure "Guide to Exterior Art and Symbolism" helps with interpretation.

On the west side of the capitol is the famed Lincoln statue. Daniel Chester French sculpted the standing sixteenth president and then collaborated with architect Henry Bacon to design the perfect backdrop. These two men would go on to create the sitting Abraham Lincoln found at the Washington, D.C. Lincoln Memorial. In front of the second Nebraska Capitol, Abraham Lincoln's statue was dedicated in 1912. Even through construction of the third capitol, the statue has remained.

Inside the Nebraska Capitol

A masterpiece from floor to ceiling, the cohesive design of this capitol is apparent. Throughout the building, Nebraska symbols are on display. All three Nebraska branches of government are here. The Nebraska governor's suite is near the north entrance. As the only unicameral one in the United

States, the state legislature is housed in a single room. The former Senate room is still used for special occasions. In the South Hall, seven justices preside over the Nebraska Supreme Court.

Visitors can ride one of two classic elevators to the fourteenth floor of this building. The central chamber displays paintings completed by Nebraska artist Stephen Roberts. Each one focuses on Nebraska history and the spirit of volunteerism. During warmer weather, the observation level decks are open. Visitors can see amazing panoramic bird's-eye views from the capitol.

MUSEUMS

Nebraska History Museum

The state's official history museum completed a major systems update in spring 2016. What resulted is a new design that allowed historians to rework displays. Currently, temporary exhibits tell about Nebraska's past. Over time, the museum plans to have permanent displays on both the second and third floors.

One purpose of this location is education. Planned family outreach events take place throughout the year. During Story Hour at the Museum, children listen to a themed Nebraska book and then participate in hands-on activities. For the adults, monthly brown bag lectures focus on certain aspects of Nebraska history.

Down the street is the Nebraska State Historical Society headquarters. This organization operates the museum and several historic sites around the state. At the Nebraska History Landmark Store, books and other Nebraska items are sold. Many items are available for online purchasing.

Lincoln Firefighting Museum

At the downtown Lincoln Fire Station is the Capital City's firefighter collection. Open daily with free admission, this large room provides a great introduction to firefighting. Included is the 1911 American LaFrance pumper, the city's first motorized fire engine. Seeing how fire equipment has progressed in safety measures is intriguing. The best part of this museum is that active firefighters themselves provide the tours. Be aware that they could have to leave in the middle to go out on a call. They have a community to protect.

Roller Skating Museum

Roller skates used to consist of boards with wheels attached. Considered the father of modern roller skating, James L. Plimpton updated the skate. His rocker version allowed skaters to steer from side to side with ease. His family's skating collection is now in Lincoln. The National Museum of Roller Skating covers two centuries of skating history.

One wall demonstrates the evolution of skating wheels. Much to visitors' delight, all the wheels spin. Glass-encased displays include skating trinkets and costumes. Relive roller rink days with videos showing artistic competitions. Along with speed skating, roller derby and roller hockey are displayed. For researchers, this location's archives are extensive.

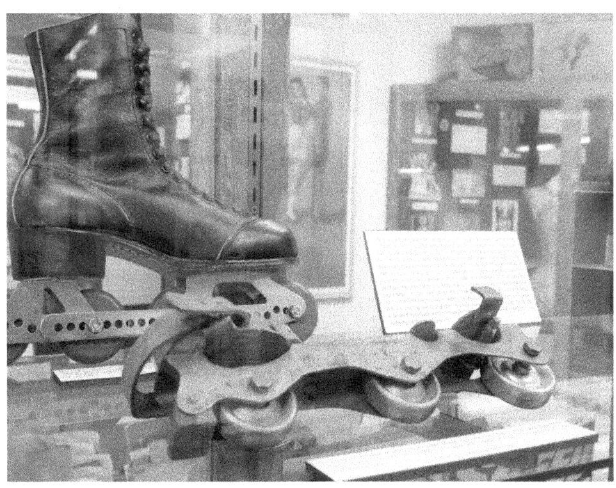

The National Museum of Roller Skating displays skating artifacts from over two centuries.

Frank H. Woods Telephone Pioneer Museum

For over a decade, one museum has sought to preserve a fading form of communication—the telephone. In 1903, Woods started the Lincoln Telephone Company. His company might have been the largest almost automatic phone system west of Chicago. Independent telephone companies were rare.

Containing telecommunication equipment from the last century, exhibits include switchboards and candlestick phones. Various telephone operator headsets show the progress of technology. Even an antique phone booth is on display. See Woods's reconstructed office, complete with his own framed photographs and actual desk.

Museum of American Speed

Although the Museum of American Speed was founded in 1992, the concept started long before. "Speedy" Bill and Joyce Smith were a part of the racing and hot rodding industry for six decades. During that time, they accumulated artifacts of personal interest, and a desire to display these historical items developed. Although the Smiths have now passed away, the family has continued their legacy.

The Smiths' collection is large in magnitude. The museum encompasses 150,000 square feet on three levels. Not everything is shown—many items are in storage. The curators want the displays to remain fluid, and exhibitions change frequently. Although some of the sections are more permanent, even some of the displayed cars are rotated. Visitors will want to return often to see the changes.

Featured in the front room are NASCAR and other racers. Many cars are well known in the racing world. The Miller-Ford Indy car became famous for losing. Modifications did not prove successful in the 1930s. A favorite stock car is the no. 21 white Mercury Montago with the red hard top built by the Woods Brothers. This car won the 1976 Daytona 500 and became a racing favorite for the next fourteen years. Besides automobiles, this room is filled with other racing souvenirs. Helmets, apparel, prints and drawings tell about this speedy pastime. Complete engines range from one cylinder to v-16 cylinders. Other component parts allow visitors to see what is under the hood.

The back wall contains the Speedway Motors collection. The 1932 Ford Sedan Reproduction of a 1960 Modified Dirt Car won sixteen consecutive races. The driver, Lloyd Beckman, rode in the center of the car. Speedy Smith mentions in his exhibit notes that his success hurt his popularity for a time. The mechanical rabbit sprint car was a collaborative design by three racers. All requested Speedway Motors to help with construction. Don Maxwell built the 4x sprint car for Speedy Smith. Various drivers saw a range of success with this car. Surrounding these cars are racing pictures, memorabilia and Smith family photographs.

The show car collection room features customized automobiles. Often based on previous models, the redesigns add another level of creativity. The collection includes "Boot Hill Express," a hot rod created by Ray Fahrner from a horse-drawn stage carriage. This wagon transported a deceased James-Younger crew member to his final resting place. Stories about the cars are on the museum website, including the fascinating tale of the 1934 Ford Cabriolet Goldbrick. Classic car enthusiasts modified these cars.

The production vehicles room features cars found in automobile showrooms. Besides the anticipated Ford Model Ts, many others are rare and unusual. The 1886 Benz Patent Motor-Wagen is the oldest vehicle. Considered coach-built, customers purchased just the chassis of the 1930 Dusenberg 4-Door Phaeton and then customized the rest. Designer Preston Tucker only built fifty-one of his Tucker Torpedo Sedans back in 1948. The room is filled with classic cars.

Smith's smaller-scale collections include soapbox derby cars, pedal cars and mini gas-powered automobiles. Even those who are not racing enthusiasts will find much to love at this location. Smith's lunchbox collection lines the stair walls. Filling one hallway's ceiling is a display of guitars. Every square foot seems to be filled with another wonder.

Volunteer curators are around to provide tours. The admission cost is justifiable for these amazing displays. Open year round, hours are limited during fall and winter.

LUX Center for the Arts

In 1889, visitors to this section of Lincoln would have actually been in Athens, Nebraska. During Lincoln's early days, several small communities were found on the outskirts of town. When Nebraska Wesleyan arrived, Athens was renamed University Place. In 1914, this Methodist community built a new town hall. After Lincoln absorbed University Place, the building became a fire station and then later a restaurant. Wesleyan professor Gladys Lux purchased the building to save it from being torn down. In 1985, the building became the home of the University Place Art Center.

This nonprofit endeavor had begun eight years prior. Originally, the center was in a house near Wesleyan. Started to teach art skills, the center also provided a gallery for students to show off their work. In 2003, the Center was renamed LUX Center for the Arts. This honored its longtime supporter, Gladys Lux, who had passed away earlier that year at age 103.

At this art center, rotating exhibits are found in four different galleries featuring local and nationally recognized artists. Art classes provide educational opportunities for all ages. Fabulous family workshops take place several times a year. Outreach programs bring hands-on art education out into the community. Artists in residence are brought to LUX from around the country. While at the center, they focus on their craft while providing enriching experiences to visitors. With the addition of its new ceramics center, LUX is continuing to add beauty to its corner of the world and beyond.

UNIVERSITY OF NEBRASKA MUSEUMS

Lester F. Larsen Tractor Test and Power Museum

Switching from horses to gasoline-powered tractors in farming should have been an easy process. Yet in the early years, skeptics were unsure of this change. Horses are reliable, but tractors also staked their claim in the industry. Beginning in 1908, the Winnipeg Industrial Exhibition staged tractor events. In 1911, the United States decided to start public tractor demonstrations as well. This annual event took place near Omaha for five years and lasted long enough to convince farmers of the merit of gasoline-powered engines.

The next tractor concerns were production standards and advertising claims. In this brand-new field, all tractors were not equal. Osceola farmer Wilmot Crozier discovered this firsthand. His 1916 Ford (no relation to the automobile) tractor was the most affordable—and the least reliable. Due to frequent breakdowns, Crozier demanded a new model. The 1917 Minneapolis Ford tractor was not any better. Exasperated by his experiences, he switched tractor companies. The Bull Tractor also failed to meet expectations. Finally, his Rumley Oil Pull exceeded its advertised performance.

Elected to the Nebraska state legislature in 1919, Crozier became a voice for agriculture. Farmers everywhere felt frustration with tractor model inconsistencies. Representative Crozier and Senator Charles Warner of Waverly helped pass a state law: the Nebraska Tractor Bill. All tractors sold in Nebraska became required to reach a certain sale standard. Essentially, tractors must perform as advertised. Replacement parts should be readily available to allow for repairs. Thus, the Nebraska Tractor Test Laboratory began. Almost one hundred years later, this location is still the only official independent tractor test lab in the Western Hemisphere.

Today, the world's first tractor test lab site is open for tours. Indoor testing is now completed at a larger facility nearby. Both the past and present labs are found at the University of Nebraska–Lincoln, East Campus. The museum sits at the end of the now-paved track. Up to thirty tractors can be seen both inside and out. A Minneapolis Ford tractor model is one of them. Displays include antique agricultural parts, engines, implements, toy tractors and a Model T Ford.

The children's area encourages them to connect to rural roots. Complete with an accessible tractor cab for climbing, children can play and learn. A scavenger hunt helps children explore the museum in a meaningful way. The museum is open Tuesdays through Fridays plus the first Saturday of each month. Groups may request to visit outside those hours. Donations are requested for admission.

International Quilt Study Center and Museum

Gathering quilts started out as a hobby for Robert and Ardis James. Over time, their collection came to contain several hundred stitched masterpieces. As they wanted their quilts to be displayed, preserved and studied, they began looking for locations willing to start a museum. The University of Nebraska–Lincoln agreed to take on this challenge. In 1997, the International Quilt Study Center and Museum began. The Jameses donated their collection to the university and the people of Nebraska. Since then, other donors have given quilts to the university as well. About a decade later, the Quilt House opened on the university's East Campus. Now the growing collection has a permanent home.

Throughout the climate-controlled galleries, exhibits rotate. Shows vary and may highlight a specific artisan or a type of quilt construction. Although some quilts are on loan, often the museum's own collection is displayed. The study center encourages research and discovery. Outside the main galleries, a designated area encourages children to explore quilts. The International Quilt Study Center and Museum hopes to teach future generations to continue this long-standing artistic tradition.

The university has two additional art museums. At the Great Plains Art Museum, people and places of the plains take center stage. The goal is also to provide research and extended learning opportunities, including symposiums. Down the street, the Sheldon Museum of Art's collection of American art is diverse. Featuring complex pieces, this museum has displayed art in Lincoln for over fifty years.

University of Nebraska State Museum of Natural History and Mueller Planetarium

Most locals call this museum Morrill Hall because the main exhibition area carries that name. Known for its massive mammoth collection, this location includes many excellent diorama displays. While some do address the origin of life, many modern-day animals are arranged by habitat. Other sections tell of Native American history. This museum presents Nebraska.

Experiential learning happens at this museum. A favorite for kids is the Discovery Zone, where they can explore the "dinosaur dig area," act on a small stage and interact with science and art. Some exhibits rotate. "Sundays with a Scientist" events reach out to the community with science. The onsite planetarium gives visitors a full dome experience.

The Lincoln Children's Zoo

Arnott Folsom wanted his community to connect with nature and animals. His donation spurred the project on, and the zoo opened in 1965. Today at the Animal Encounter Stage, zookeepers show animals in a new way. At the Humboldt Penguin exhibit, kids count how many fish are eaten during the shows and win train rides. From the beginning, the Iron Horse Railroad has been a family favorite. With the Zoofari campaign, Nebraska comedian Larry the Cable Guy uses animals as outreach. His zoo videos are shown at children's hospitals around the country. The "Love Your Zoo" campaign is helping this location to expand. In 2019, four additional exhibits will open.

Saline Wetlands

Salt was one contributing factor in moving the capital to Lincoln. Although this industry never proved to be commercially productive, salt is still making an impact. Around the edges of the city are thirteen saline wetlands. These areas are open for public exploration.

Denton Spring Creek Prairie Audubon Center

Located several miles west of Lincoln is a grassland oasis. An area set apart for exploring the best Nebraska nature has to offer, this is the perfect spot for a family outing. Mowed paths make hiking a bit easier, but the adventurous can forge their own trails. In fact, to experience the wagon rut paths of the early pioneers, leaving the maintained trails is necessary. Actual wagon tracks are not visible; instead, the repeated movement of wagons eroded the land. Prairie grass filled in the gaps, and the grooves and indentations are felt even underneath shoes. Particularly in late summer, this trek can be challenging in the tall grasses. Near the small pond, turtles often sun themselves on chunky logs.

To encourage observation, backpacks of various themes are available to check out. In the nature-themed sack, journals and pencils are provided to chronicle plants and animals. Magnifying glasses and other study tools are also included.

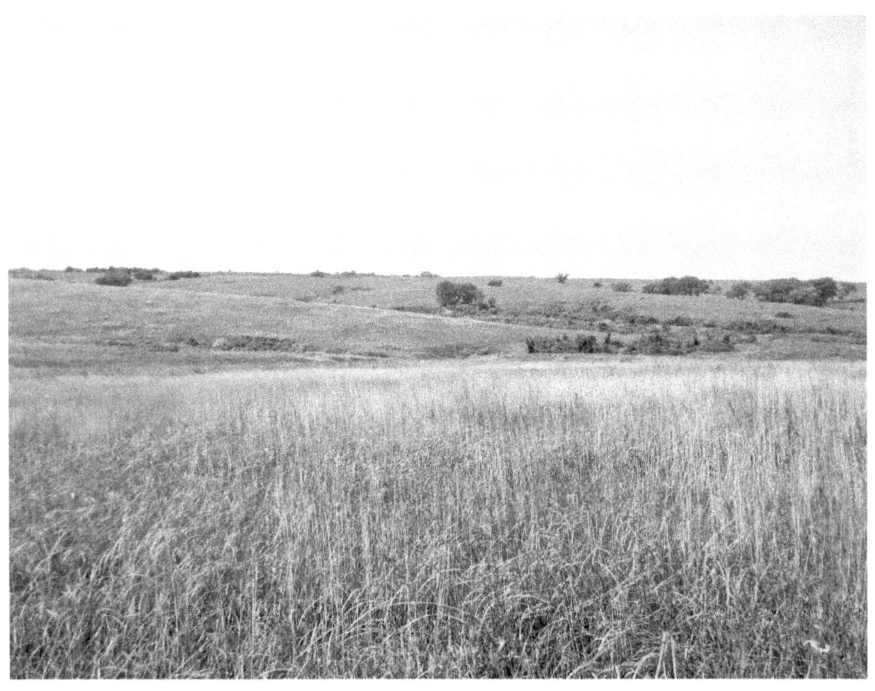

Spring Creek Prairie Audubon Center, found at the former Nebraska City–Fort Kearny Oregon Trail cutoff point, contains unplowed prairie.

2
PIONEER REGION

Go west young man, and grow up with the country.
—John B.L. Soule, Terre Haute Express *1851 editorial*

This is pioneer country. Overflowing from nearby Kansas, Missouri and Iowa, people made their way here. Nebraska's original settlers established the state's direction.

Nebraska City

When Nebraska became a territory in 1854, Nebraska City became a town. One of the oldest settlements, its proximity to the Missouri River accelerated growth. Freighting was king. In various avenues, Nebraska City still thrives.

Missouri River Basin Lewis & Clark Center

An authentic life-sized outdoor keelboat reproduction is at this museum's entrance. From the entrance, all the displays help visitors experience the Louisiana Purchase expedition. A reproduction of Seaman, Lewis's Newfoundland dog, commands the small boat. An expedition-style tent holds replicated supplies, including a sextant, a blacksmith forge and even medicinal supplies.

Exhibits focus on scientific discoveries. Throughout their thirty-month expedition, Lewis, Clark and their crew made many finds. They documented 178 varieties of plants and identified 122 new animals. All of the discovered plants and animals are on display. In honor of prairie dogs, pretend tunnels wind through part of the basement. Just like the prairie dogs hid from Lewis and Clark, guests can hide, too. Although Lewis and Clark flooded the tunnels to get the prairie dogs to come, simply calling your kids out is a better option.

Outside, this nature focus continues with waiting historic trails. Two paths lead to reproduction buildings, a Pawnee Indian earth lodge and a smaller Fort Mandan. Overlooking the Missouri River, visitors can almost imagine what traveling with Lewis and Clark would have been like long ago.

Nebraska City Firefighter's Museum

The oldest fire department in the state of Nebraska displays the state's progression in firefighting. Dating back to 1856, leather buckets were used by the citizens' bucket brigade. On display are an 1861 Demming hand pump, an 1865 ladder wagon and the original company hose carts. The showpiece of the museum is the rare 1881 button steamer. Various motorized fire apparatus are included as well. The 1926 and 1938 Seagraves trucks made fighting fire in Nebraska City a bit easier. Visitors can see the advancements in water transportation and suppression systems. Also noteworthy is the collection of firefighting patches. Certain insignias are from far beyond Nebraska City. Open April through October, this museum also celebrates the spirit of volunteerism.

Nebraska City and the Underground Railroad

Nebraska became a state two years after the Civil War ended. Presumably, slavery should not have been an issue. Yet because of bordering Missouri, slavery had an impact. The Underground Railroad passed through Nebraska Territory borders. By following the Missouri River, slaves could start on the path to freedom. Once arriving at Nebraska City, the fugitive could cross into the free state of Iowa. Past Chicago and into Canada, freedom awaited. Exactly how many slaves used this route is impossible to determine.

The Mayhew Cabin in Nebraska City, along with John Brown's Cave, was a small Underground Railroad station. The Mayhew family relocated from Ohio to a log cabin near the Missouri River. Although Nebraska's early census only counted ten slaves, this bothered antislavery Mrs. Mayhew and her brother, John Kagi, who lived with them for several months. The tunnel beneath their cabin provided the perfect passageway for helping slaves escape.

Kagi was a companion of John Brown, the man who would eventually lead a raid on Harpers Ferry. His bold slavery protests helped catapult the nation into the Civil War. Records are unclear if Brown visited Kagi in Nebraska, but the underground cave bears Brown's name. The Underground Railroad involved secrecy. Yet proof does exist that at least one dozen fleeing slaves passed underneath the cabin at one point, stopping long enough to eat breakfast.

Today, visitors can tour the small Mayhew Cabin and see a reproduction of the cave. On site, relocated historical buildings form a village. Included is one of the first African American churches west of the Missouri River. This museum brings the reality of slavery to life. Documenting Nebraska's small part in rescuing slaves is its mission.

J. STERLING MORTON AND ARBOR DAY

Nebraska City's Legacy of Trees

Arbor Day…which has already transplanted itself…to every state in the American Union and has even been adopted in foreign lands…is not like other holidays. Each of those reposes on the past while Arbor Day proposes for the future.

—J. Sterling Morton, Arbor Day founder

When J. Sterling Morton and his family moved to Nebraska from Detroit, he became the editor of the local *Nebraska City News*. Stressing the importance of agriculture and agronomy became part of the paper's purpose. Morton's involvement in local and state government gave him a voice of influence.

Later, as Nebraska Territory secretary of agriculture, Morton encouraged planting. Trees would help stop erosion and provide windbreaks. Five years after Nebraska's statehood, Morton had a proposal. At a State Board of Agriculture meeting, he suggested a tree-planting holiday. On April 10, 1872, volunteers planted around one million trees statewide. Within a decade, Arbor Day was celebrated around the United States. Although Morton died long ago, his ecological influence is still felt worldwide.

Arbor Lodge State Historical Park

The Mortons' Nebraska City home, initially a four-room frame house, is open for tours. Both Sterling and his son, Joy, completed expansions. Arbor Lodge now has fifty-two rooms. Besides intricate woodwork, the home features many of the family's Victorian- and Empire-style furnishings. One unique addition is the basement one-lane bowling alley. Both a log cabin and the carriage house are open for exploration. Plants still grow in the terraced Italian-style gardens and onsite greenhouse.

Arbor Day Farm

Tree Adventure and Discovery Rides

Connecting visitors to the outdoors is the purpose of this center. All are encouraged to explore the multiple paved and wood-chipped paths winding through the property. Along the way, hikers can guess which animals' footprints are preserved. With bridges to cross and fifty-foot-tall treehouse ladders to climb, adventures await. Inside the treehouse cabin, interactive displays await the curious.

Two outdoor classrooms bring exploratory learning to life. Giant marimbas sound off. Movable giant scarves make excellent swings. Sticks are stacked and ready for structure building. At the outdoor stage are many youthful performances, and the open play concept is effective.

The indoor Woodland Pavilion lets guests wander around a small indoor forest. Through visual displays, the impact of Arbor Day in Nebraska and worldwide is apparent. A short documentary, *Trees in the Movies*, is fun to watch.

From April to November, guests can enjoy a wagon Discovery Ride. This one-hour excursion takes visitors to nature in a new way. Depending on the time of year, different aspects are highlighted.

The greenhouses are often open to visitors. Many items produced at the farm, including apple cider and signature wines, are sold at the Apple House Market next door. The Pie Garden Café is a place to refuel after hiking. Although the operating hours are shorter during late fall into winter, Arbor Day Farm is open year round. Admission is charged for some areas. During the fall, the Applejack Festival provides a fun time to visit Nebraska City.

AN ENCHANTED ARBORETUM

In 2010, Nebraska City leaders decided to enhance their town. Using trees as their focus, a public art project began. Local and outside artists painted tree statues with purposeful designs. In the end, twenty-five six-foot sculptures were completed. Although the statues were later auctioned off, many were placed around town. All sculptures can be seen online.

KREGEL WINDMILL FACTORY MUSEUM AND MORE

In 1903, the Kregel Manufacturing Factory moved to Central Avenue. For the next forty years, it continued to make Eli Windmills. As the windmills were only sold to individuals, the factory did not have a nationwide presence. Rarely are any found more than a few hundred miles away. Once materials became scarce in World War II, the small factory switched to performing repairs. In 1991, the shop closed for good. This could have been the end of the story.

Upon inheriting the building, some Kregel relatives realized this location was significant. Little had been updated in the windmill factory during the previous ninety years. Wall shelves were crammed with tools and parts; even all the business paperwork was still spread out. Twenty original machines were around the shop. This factory from another time had a story to tell.

Further research substantiated the need to preserve the site. The Kregel Windmill Factory's original equipment is intact. No other small-scale windmill manufacturing operations can make that claim. Making this

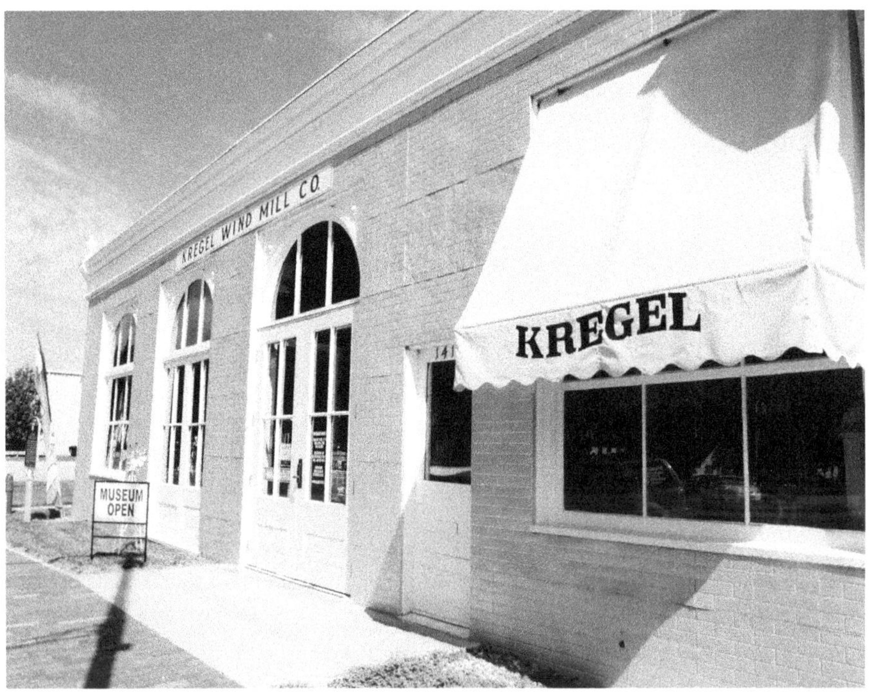

With intact original equipment and supplies, the Kregel Windmill Factory Museum is a treasure-trove of unexpected items.

building acceptable for public tours was quite an undertaking because the original Kregel owners had kept almost everything.

Maintaining authenticity while still allowing room for tourists was challenging. Besides the factory element, the Kregel Windmill Factory Museum wants to portray often-forgotten values to visitors. Industriousness, resourcefulness and resiliency are promoted. Hard work mattered. Everything was kept, just in case. This factory survived despite limitations. The life lessons that can be learned from a room overflowing with manufacturing equipment and supplies are amazing.

Many other Nebraska City locations are worth visiting. The Old Freighter's Museum and Nelson House capture town history. So does the Civil War Veteran's Museum at GAR Hall. Tour the Wildwood Historic House, the Barn Art Gallery and Victoria Garden. Kimmel-Harding-Nelson Center features the arts. The River County Nature Center promotes exploration, and the Titan Toy Museum is a blast from the past.

Nemaha County

One of Nebraska's original nine counties, Nemaha County is noteworthy. To contain local history, three Auburn museum buildings were needed. Nearby is Nebraska's oldest college. Started in 1867 as a teacher training school, Peru State College has continued to grow and expand.

Brownville

In 1854, the Nebraska Territory opened to settlers. Soon after, Richard Brown paddled across the Missouri River to stake his claim, and he built his cabin's foundation that very day. Brownville became an official town in 1856 and continues to build on that history.

Brownville flourished right away. One early resident was Robert W. Furnas. This journalist brought along the first newspaper presses and started publishing the *Nebraska Advertiser* on June 7, 1856. As a proclaimed agriculturalist, Furnas planted some area trees and plants. After his stint as a Civil War colonel, Furnas was an Omaha Indian Agency representative. From 1873 to 1875, he served one term as Nebraska governor. Today, his historic home is open for tours. Besides Furnas family exhibits, displays feature Brownville history. Nearby is the Governor Furnas Arboretum. All the trees in this shady spot are identified for visitors strolling through.

The Brownville Historical Society keeps the past alive. Three other historic Brownville homes are open for tours. The Carson House, home of the first banker, and its accompanying carriage house feature early town life. Captain Bailey House holds an eclectic collection of clothing, furniture and toys. Civil War artifacts displayed are in honor of its former owner. Once located in the country, the Didier Log Cabin is now in a Brownville Park. Current town residents reconstructed the cabin in the same dimensions using similar materials.

The town museums explore local history too. The Railroad Museum presents the train's impact. Once renovations are complete, the Wheel Museum will be all about movement. From surreys to fishing boats, exhibits share how people traveled in and out of town. Civil War cannons are also displayed. Walk through Dr. Spurgin's Dental Office to see tools and oddities displayed behind glass.

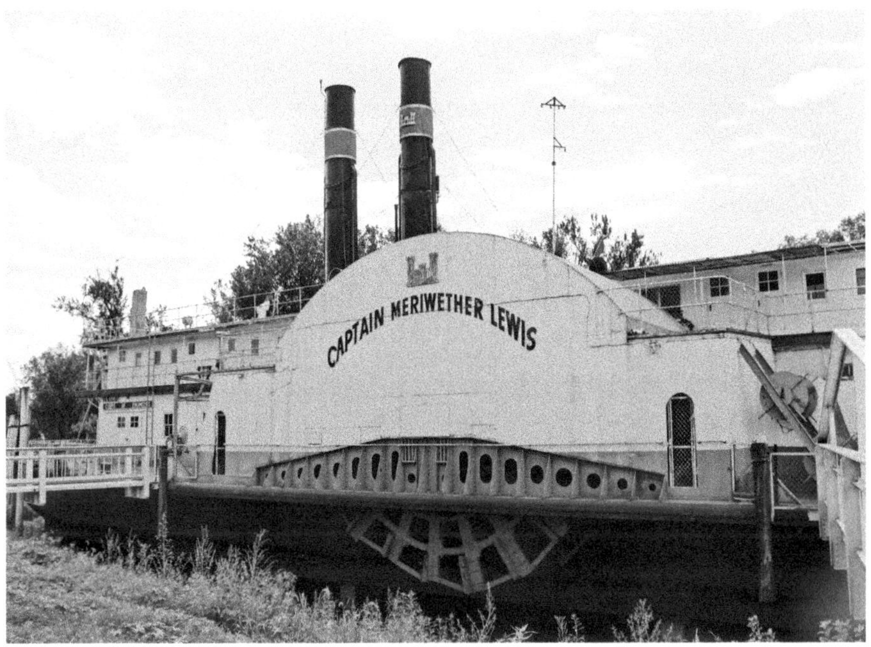

The *Captain Meriwether Lewis* dustpan dredge rests beside the Missouri, the river it once cleared.

Outside of town sits the *Captain Meriwether Lewis* side-wheeler dredge boat. This large vessel channeled the Missouri River to keep it navigable from 1931 to 1976. Complete with a galley and sailors' quarters, visitors can see into life on a boat. Part of the space tells about Missouri River history.

With world-class productions, Brownville is a reputable artistic destination. At the Concert Hall, the Brownville Fine Arts Association brings Broadway to Nebraska. Throughout the season, New York stars perform in Nebraska. A former church building is now the Brownville Theater. Many theater majors spend their summer acting in town. Because acting and technical participation are both required, this is a true repertory theater. Performances are often musical or farcical in nature.

Americana art is explored in Brownville. The Flatwater Folk Art Museum's unique pieces include paint-by-number. Even gold replica Statue of Liberty sculptures and wooden duck decoys are displayed. Down the street, the Schoolhouse Art Gallery features quilts, pottery, paintings and books. Thomas Palmerton's western and wildlife bronzes are available at his

Palmerton Gallery. Rounding out the art experience in Brownville is New Earth Clay Pottery.

Brownville offers travelers unique lodging at the River Inn Resort. Eighteen rooms are available in the floating bed-and-breakfast. The *Spirit of Brownville* riverboat offers dinner cruises. To visit Brownville, travelers should plan ahead. Many locations are only open during seasonal weekends, and some do charge admission.

INDIAN CAVE STATE PARK NEAR SCHUBERT

Long ago, Native Americans left a petroglyph record of their presence. From the boardwalk, visitors can look into the cave at these drawings. On site is the restored schoolhouse and general store from the former river town of St. Deroin. During living history weekends, old-time crafts and traditions take place. Miles of hiking and equestrian trails are accessible at this hilly location. To enter, a state park permit is required.

JOHN PHILIP FALTER MUSEUM IN FALLS CITY

In the small town of Falls City, Nebraska, Americana shines. At a beautiful historic building, many of the best *Saturday Evening Post* original covers are on display. The artist responsible is John Philip Falter. Growing up in this area of southeast Nebraska gave Falter a unique viewpoint. His surroundings inspired him. Rural life, pioneers and Native Americans would become frequent artwork themes in his later years. After graduating from Falls City in 1928, Falter's education continued at the Kansas City Art Institute. Later, a provided scholarship allowed him to attend the New York City Arts Student League.

During the Great Depression, many prospective illustrators set up studios in coastal New York. Here Falter started illustrating advertisements. Following in his role model Norman Rockwell's footsteps came naturally to him. In 1943, thirty-three-year-old John Philip Falter's dream came true. His first *Saturday Evening Post* cover featured Benjamin Franklin. Falter would create a total of 129 covers and became the second most prolific *Saturday Evening Post* illustrator.

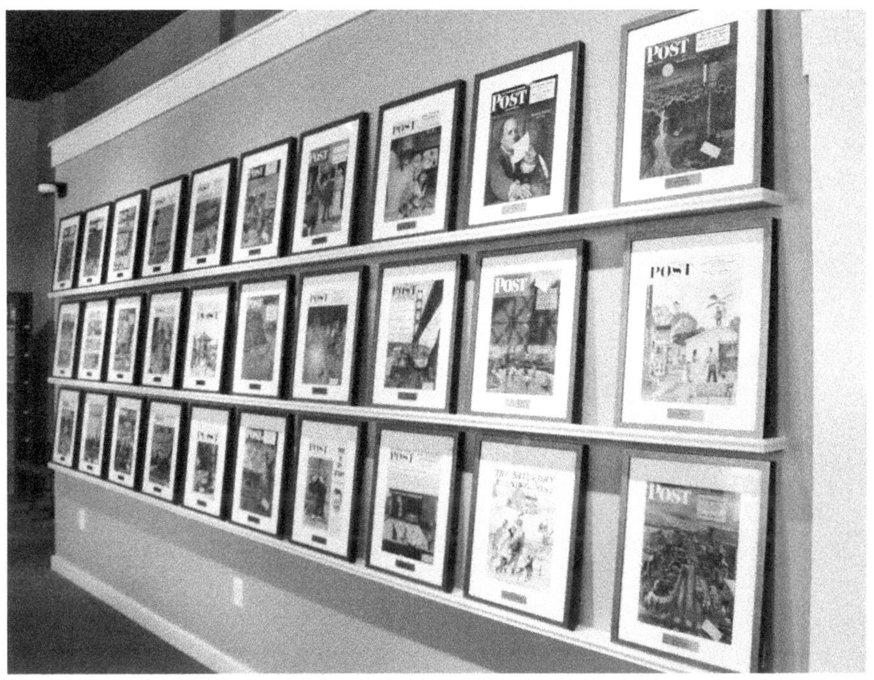

The John Philip Falter Museum shows off many of his *Saturday Evening Post* covers.

Throughout the years, Falter did not forget Falls City. Familiar faces and hometown places are in his drawings, and he returned to the area several times to keep in touch. After Falter passed away in 1982, Falls City citizens talked about honoring his work. Thirty-two years later, the time arrived. In May 2015, the John Philip Falter Museum was officially open. The town brought to life in Falter's paintings would now bring his artwork back to life.

The museum tells Falter's story in multiple ways. A replica of his Philadelphia studio is on loan from the Nebraska State Historical Society; all his *Saturday Evening Post* covers are displayed on a rotating basis. Other masterpieces are also framed for viewing. To see this wonderful artwork collection, contact the curator for an appointment. The number is found on the John Philip Falter Museum website.

Pawnee County

Harold Lloyd never expected his small Burchard home to become a museum. Between 1915 and 1919, this Nebraskan starred in two hundred silent films. Most were comedies, complete with daredevil acrobatics that he completed without a stunt man. Lloyd's most famous film was *Safety Last*. Nearby in Table Rock, a museum and five other buildings contain county historical displays. To visit these locations, appointments are necessary.

Gage County Historical Sites

Drought and grasshoppers were not kind to early Nebraska farmers. Defeated, many headed back east. Elijah Filley knew departing neighbors would limit his own prairie days. By paying his neighbors to help build a barn, they could still afford to homestead. In 1874, Filley and friends built a three-story limestone structure that still stands today. Although outdoor photographs are always possible, the barn is only open during periodic Living History days.

Located in the former Beatrice 1906 Burlington-Northern depot, the Gage County Museum displays local history. Exhibits focus on the county's railroad, industry, medical and agricultural aspects and tell of local residents. One such person is John Fulton, who was an early Hollywood movie special-effects artist. This museum closes during wintertime.

The Nebraska Baseball Hall of Fame in Beatrice

Since 2012, this Beatrice location has featured equipment and memorabilia from Nebraska's baseball inductees. Over a century of history is explained through articles and photographs. This developing museum gives historical insight into Nebraska's part in America's favorite pastime. To visit, contact the museum in advance.

THE HOMESTEAD NATIONAL MONUMENT OF AMERICA NEAR BEATRICE

An allusion has been made to the Homestead Law. I think it worthy of consideration, and that the wild lands of the country should be distributed so that every man should have the means and opportunity of benefitting his condition.
—President Abraham Lincoln, February 12, 1861

Wanting to settle the western United States, President Abraham Lincoln encouraged Congress to pass four pivotal pieces of legislation. One law directly affected the Nebraska Territory. The Homestead Act allowed settlers to claim 160 acres for a small paperwork fee. After living at their homestead site and making improvements for a set time, that land would be theirs permanently.

The Homestead Act became an official law on January 1, 1863. Right after midnight, Nebraskan Daniel Freeman was the first to file his claim. The Brownville land office office stayed open for him. Freeman's 160 acres were located outside of the new town of Beatrice, and he and various family members would live there for almost seventy years. At the site of his claim now stands the National Park Service's Homestead National Monument.

Starting with the precisely one-acre parking lot, the Homestead Act's impact is evident. Lining the walkway are thirty bronze maps. This Living Wall represents the states that participated in the Homestead movement. Even the Heritage Center's roof resembles a bottom plow used to break hardened sod.

Inside, interactive exhibits demonstrate the influence of the Homestead Act. From 1863 to 1976, millions of claims were filed. The last claim was staked in Alaska. The exhibits present homesteading from many perspectives. From agricultural revolution to preservation of both land and people, the act's influence is far reaching. A scavenger hunt engages younger visitors. Completed papers earn elementary kids Junior Ranger badges.

South of the Heritage Center is the Palmer-Epard cabin, once located fourteen miles northeast. The Palmers lived here first. Their fourteen- by sixteen-foot cabin was considered luxurious. At one time, a lean-to added space. After the Palmers, the Epards lived in the cabin for almost forty years. In 1950, the building became monument property. Since then, this sturdy cabin has survived several moves of its own. Board by board, the cabin has been reassembled several times. Since 2009, the cabin has sat near the Heritage Center.

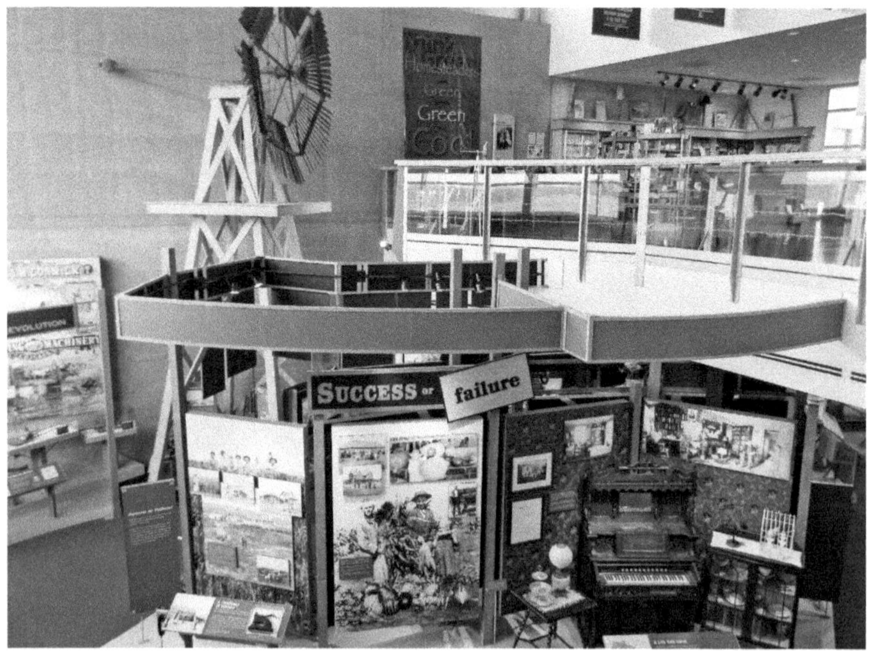

The Homestead National Monument of America covers all facets of the Homestead Act.

Down the road is the official Education Center. Hands-on crafts and living history demonstrations are scheduled often. Displays reflect the agricultural component of homesteading. The restored 1870s District no. 21 Freeman School testifies to the area's commitment to education. This school had shipped desks in from Indiana and even provided textbooks.

If visitors stay indoors, they will miss the beauty of Homestead National Monument of America. Guests can trek into the tall-grass prairie or follow cellphone audio tours. By utilizing GPS equipment, visitors can find two geocaching spots. Earth caching is also possible. Clues lead to the real treasure: the land.

Other County Attractions

Take Highway 12 toward Odell to see Krider Hill. Once home to the Otoe tribe, the panoramic views of the prairie are breathtaking. Featuring a one-hundred-foot mural explaining transportation history, Odell's Old West

Trails Center focuses on travel. Included in this former town bank are local history displays. In addition, the Wymore Train Station Museum is open by appointment. Near Lanham and the Kansas border, an Oregon Trail Marker pays tribute to the 300,000-plus westward pioneers.

ROCK CREEK STATION NEAR FAIRBURY

On their way to Oregon or California, pioneers made their way past the Rock Creek Station. In 1867, this location became pivotal. Both stagecoaches and the Pony Express stopped here. Four years later, this spot became cemented in Wild West folklore. Although David McCanles is an unfamiliar name, James Butler Hickok is more notorious. One sweltering July day caused tempers to flare, and James became Wild Bill Hickok, with McCanles his first gunfight victim.

Today, the Rock Creek Station interpretive center is open during the summer. On display are excavated items from this location, and volunteers reconstructed the Pony Express barn, bunkhouse and several cabins. Four miles of hiking trails present the prairie and even include rut indents left by passing wagons.

MORE SOUTHEAST NEBRASKA HIGHLIGHTS

Going toward central Nebraska, detour through Hebron. The world's largest porch swing provides the perfect photo opportunity for you and a dozen of your closest friends. Nearby is Superior, the Victorian capital of Nebraska. Many of the town's homes feature this ornate architecture style.

AURORA

Pioneers in Farming and in Flash Photography

Although sod houses once filled the prairie, few remain. Before Aurora's Plainsman Museum opened in 1976, volunteers constructed an authentic indoor sod house. For years, materials from an area 1850 log cabin were stored in a barn. Now that sod house, reconstructed cabin and a 1910 house help visitors step back in time. Along the re-created boardwalk are early Hamilton County shops. This museum contains over thirty thousand historical items donated by local residents. Some of these are farming tools and implements found in the separate agricultural building. As my mom grew up in this area, this museum represents my family history.

Behind the main exhibit hall, additional historical buildings were moved on site. The Fairview District 66 schoolhouse was once southwest of town. When Civil War general Delavan Bates moved to Aurora, he built the fine frame house on the property. The Grieser Blacksmith Shop, now operational again, was once in Hampton. On occasion, these three buildings are brought to life by volunteers. With such a small staff, this museum relies on the community. Thanks to strong local support, the Plainsman will be telling the stories of the past long into the future.

A premier science center is an unusual find in a Nebraska small town. Since the stroboscope inventor's hometown is Aurora, the Edgerton Explorit Center's location makes sense. After high school, Harold "Doc" Edgerton went to the University of Nebraska–Lincoln before studying and eventually

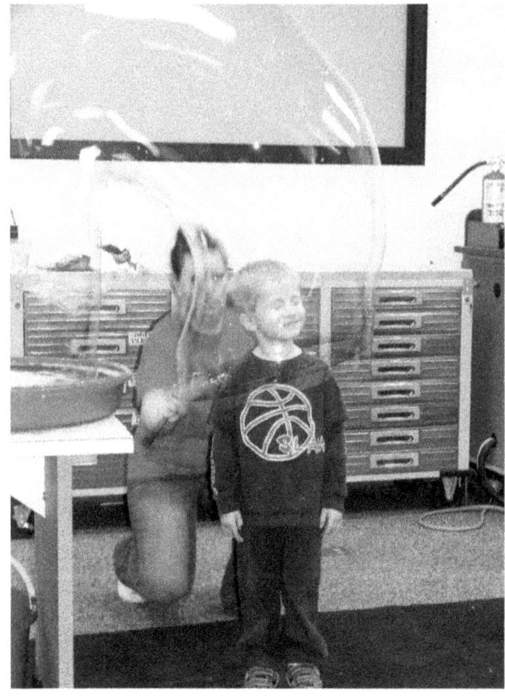

During science demonstrations at Edgerton Explorit Center, audience participation might include being inside a giant bubble.

teaching at MIT. *National Geographic* gave Edgerton more research grants than any other scientist or researcher. Even today he is considered to be one of the top inventors of the twentieth century. Known as Papa Flash, many of Edgerton's famous photographs are displayed at the Explorit Center.

Started in 1995, the Edgerton Explorit Center offers children interactive science experiences. In a room full of gadgets, kids play to learn. Staff educators' science presentations use the strobe light and common household items. Far-away schools can pay to have the museum come to them, as "Edgerton on the Move" offers various presentation options.

Prairie Plains Resource Institute

In 1980, the Prairie Plains Resource Institute was founded in Aurora. Its mission was to preserve what remained of native prairies in Nebraska. Soon, a secondary need became apparent. Declining prairies needed to be restored, and research would also help that quest. Because of its efforts, the institute would become a pioneer in the field of prairie and wetland restoration in Nebraska.

Over time, the Prairie Plains Resource Institute has acquired eight preserves. Each one contains at least a portion of native prairie, and some also include cropland. At some of the locations, grazing animals roam the property. While people can visit most of the properties, caution is needed. Everyone should avoid direct interaction with domestic or wild animals, and remember to leave the land as you found it.

Four of the prairie preserves are found near Aurora. The remaining four are throughout the state. Organized by geographical location, each of these will be mentioned in later chapters.

The first preserve, a donation of six acres by Wilma Aalborg in 1983, is located on the eastern edge of Aurora. Combining her six-acre creek portion with land leased from the town resulted in the Lincoln Creek Prairie and Trail. Although seventeen acres seems like a small area, this accessible location is frequently used by the community. Runners and bikers experience the prairie while they exercise. The institute also has restored some prairie grass along some creek corridor land.

Southeast of Aurora is the Marie Ratzlaff Prairie Preserve. This forty-acre location is a typical tall-grass prairie. Nearly one hundred native prairie plant species thrive at this location. Hikers are welcome.

Two additional Prairie Plains properties are near Marquette. The Sherman Ranch is the latest preserve acquisition. To make this possible, many individuals and organizations, including the Nebraska Environmental Trust, contributed. This 650-acre preserve includes over a mile of Platte River frontage on its northern border. Saddle clubs enjoy riding at this location. Before visiting, checking with the Prairie Plains first to find out access and usage is strongly recommended.

Nearby is the Gjerloff Prairie. Purchased from the Griffith family with a Nebraska Environmental Trust grant, this 390-acre site includes a half mile of Platte River frontage. Bluffs are throughout this preserve as well. Mowed trails invite hikers to explore the beautiful loess hills bluffs prairie.

At this location, the Charles L. Whitney Education Center is under construction. The restored barn will include lab space, a library, conference rooms and activity space. This long-awaited building will soon become the center of all Prairie Plains educational programs.

The Prairie Plains has been purposefully educating area students for over twenty-five years. All four Aurora-area preserves are used as a part of the institute's learning programs. The Prairie Plains offers day camps for two different age groups.

SOAR (Summer Orientation About Rivers) events offer two weeklong day camps for third through sixth graders. Along with high school peer leaders, kids explore natural and historic areas. For older students in grades seven through nine, the Youth Naturalist program takes outdoor learning to the next level. Throughout this weeklong event, students learn how to protect and care for area ecosystems. Participation is limited to fifteen students, so those interested should apply early for this opportunity.

As for other educational options, the institute hopes that private, public and homeschoolers will all make use of the properties. To make arrangements for any planned group outings, please call the Prairie Plains Resource Institute in advance. Employees can also inform future visitors about upcoming opportunities that allow volunteers to participate in land stewardship activities.

York County

Wessels Living History Farm

David Wessels had a dream, one he asked his friends to fulfill. Upon his death, Wessels stipulated part of his estate was for starting a living history farm. Tasked with carrying out his bequest, the York Community Foundation investigated similar projects and spent five years developing a plan. Re-creating a 1920s Nebraska farm became the mission.

Just south of Interstate 80 at York, 145 acres were purchased, but the empty land needed to become a farm. In 2002, a former Wessels house moved about fourteen miles to settle into its new home. A Shelby resident donated a typical 1920s red timber barn. Other buildings include a church, a machine shed, a chicken coop and a school. Hands-on history events happen often. On the Wessels Living History Farm educational website, early Nebraska farming is explored.

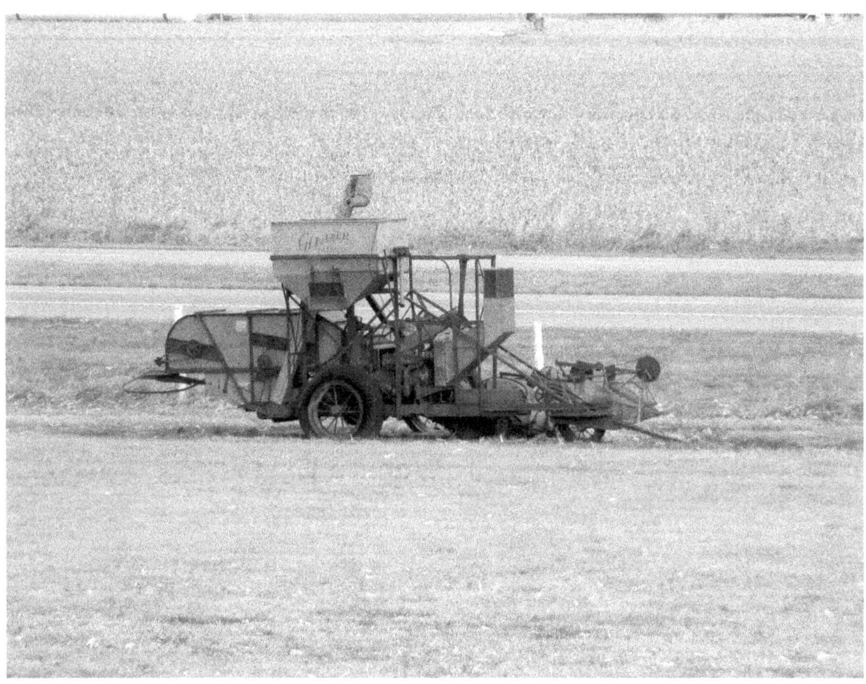

This antique gleaner is part of Wessels Living History Farm agricultural collection.

Lee's Legendary Marbles

From outside, this location off the York interstate exit seems like a common thrift-style shop. Yet this store could almost be a museum. Lining the store shelves are jars filled with about one million marbles. According to the owner, he was rather good at marbles growing up. Playing for keeps started his collection. Some marbles are for sale and make wonderful small souvenirs.

Clayton Museum of Ancient History

Down the road is another type of history. Since Nebraska is only 150 years old, this state is not synonymous with long-ago history. When Foster Stanback donated his collection of ancient artifacts to York College, this changed. Through the efforts of many, the Clayton Museum of Ancient History opened on the college campus in 2015. The Midwest meets the world. Now visitors can connect with other historic cultures in a meaningful way.

Fillmore County

At first, the Fairmont Creamery made butter. Once dairy production started in the 1880s, the creamery's yield went far beyond the state's borders. Later known as Fairmont Foods, the company outgrew its original brick office. That structure became the medical clinic for three different Dr. Ashbys. Now the Fillmore County Museum is found inside this building and inside the former town drugstore.

To organize thousands of donated items, volunteers set up booths. Many represent early careers. A millinery displays historic hats. The telephone dispatch center appears ready to make a call. Even original optometry equipment is on display. At first, early education was not a part of the museum. Local school kids collected pennies, and then a grant matched their efforts. Now a one-room schoolhouse is a part of the experience. One day each May, a local teaches area students about pioneer life. Other community members also provide hands-on history lessons.

Visiting Fairmont during Old Settlers Days is recommended. Locals transform into early town residents. Craftsmen braid rope, and volunteers make cheese. The town airs its not-so-dirty laundry, demonstrating how the washing process has changed. At the museum's authentic soda fountain, thirsty patrons can order old-fashioned drinks. Donations allow the museum to continue sharing community history.

Near Fairmont, former farm fields played a critical role during World War II. Crucial aviation training happened at the Fairmont Army Base, one of twelve Nebraska army airfield bases. During the time of operation, over three thousand soldiers and support staff lived on site. At one time, the base included almost two thousand acres. Now army veterans occasionally have reunions here. Former World War II planes add to that experience. To see airfield displays or to make tour arrangements, visit the Fillmore County Museum.

Fairmont Army Airfield is still in use today. Not all hangars are standing, but the base is still hospitable. Due to full automation, pilots can land planes day or night. As it is a central location, many have refueled or rested here.

Saline County

Named for area salt deposits, Saline County formed during the first Nebraska territorial legislature session. In the town seat, the Wilber Czech Museum celebrates local cultural heritage. Down the road, Dorchester hosts two county museums. When railroad lights are blinking, the Saline Depot Museum is open and ready to provide a railroad education. During the summer, Rentschler Farmstead gives tours highlighting the past. Featuring fourteen significant historic buildings, the farm shows the transitions made in farming over the last century.

At the former Bickle homestead in Crete, the 1870s frame house has thick walls. Upon closer examination, evidence confirms that thrifty builders constructed around the initial 1864 log cabin. On these grounds, the Crete Heritage Society preserves local history. Besides an early barn, the former Saline County District One Star School is open for tours. The Benne Memorial Museum has many local items, including an original theater curtain that features ads from early businesses.

SEWARD COUNTY

Seward is considered Nebraska's Fourth of July city. Since Nebraska's beginnings, the town has hosted a town-wide patriotic celebration. For the past 140 years and counting, the community has honored America each year. On the Fourth, the town population almost triples. About forty thousand people come to Seward for parades and parties.

BUTLER COUNTY

At the Bone Creek Museum of Agrarian Art, displays connect to land and fields. This exclusively agrarian art theme is rare. The Butler County Arts Council felt community visual art opportunities were lacking. Led by volunteer administrator Anna Nolan (Covault), the council began the nonprofit David City museum in 2007.

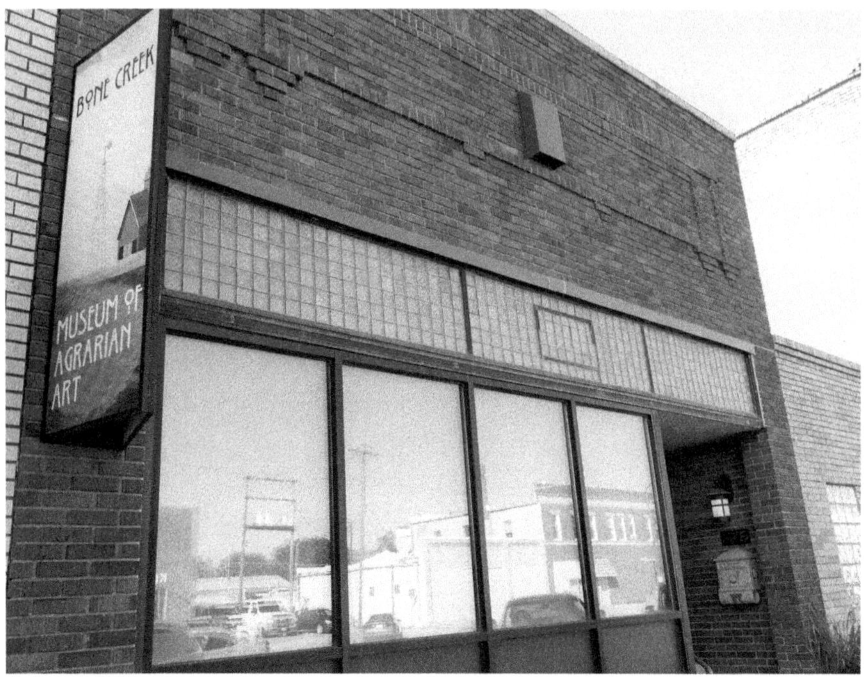

Highlighting the land is the Bone Creek Museum of Agrarian Art's mission.

David City native Dale Nichols is a premier regionalist. His art often included barns and farm life scenes. Many of Nichols's pieces are displayed as a part of the museum's permanent collection. Throughout the year, rotating exhibits and workshops focus on particular themes. Using art to connect people to the land is the mission of this museum.

3
LEWIS AND CLARK REGION

Looking for room to expand, President Thomas Jefferson purchased land from France. Almost doubling the area of the United States, the 1803 Louisiana Purchase was a bargain. At the time, few white men had seen the land. Per the president's request, Meriwether Lewis and William Clark set out on a journey to discover more about the purchased land. Following the edge of the Missouri River, the Corps of Discovery encountered what would someday be a part of Nebraska. Today, northeast Nebraska is still considered Lewis and Clark country.

Burt County

The town of Tekamah celebrates history. Not only do residents memorialize the route that Lewis and Clark once took near the community, they also relish in their own personal part in the past. Two former homes keep the town's rich history alive.

When Jack and Suzanne Bryant donated their home to the city, the goal was to "keep the past alive in the present." Their personal patriarch was none other Colonel Benjamin R. Folsom, the town founder. Visitors can envision the town through the eyes of early residents.

The Burt County Museum has a unique home. On three levels, the E.C. Houston House showcases history. From classic paintings to collectibles, treasures are everywhere. The young at heart will love the assortment of vintage toys. The adjacent C.D. Houston House, or East House continues the historical theme. Pioneers are highlighted.

COLUMBUS

All who come to Columbus are invited to visit, explore and experience all the town has to offer. An immense mural found on the edge of downtown's Frankfort Square tells about Columbus's beginnings. *Discovering the Colorful History of Columbus* captures 150 years of town history. Working backward from 2006, the layers of time are visually peeled away, back all the way to the town's founding on May 28, 1856. Pictures highlight eight aspects that have made Columbus great.

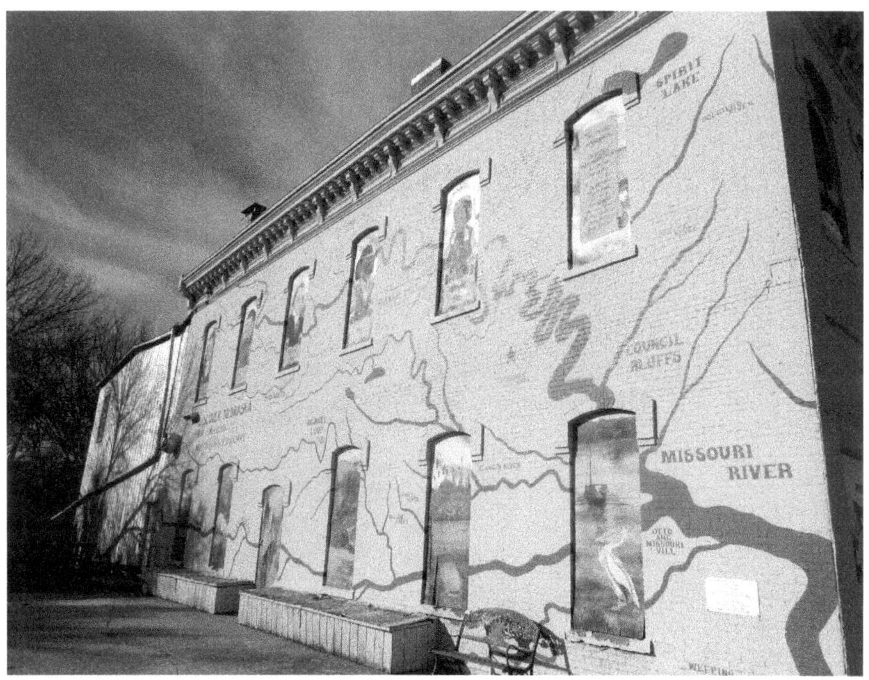

Where Highways 75 and 32 meet, this 1,560-square-foot mural in Tekamah shows Lewis and Clark's path through Nebraska. *Photo by Tim Trudell.*

PAWNEE PARK

Honoring History through Bells and Boats

Near the entrance to Pawnee Park, ten former area church bells peal out every fifteen minutes. The Quincentenary Belltower debuted in 1992. Although Columbus was named for the Ohio town, this Nebraska community wanted to honor the early American explorer. Christopher Columbus's arrival to the New World five hundred years prior deserved a celebratory display. Designer Craig Dunham's open transparency concept provides the perfect backdrop to honor the discoverer.

Farther into the park, more history is portrayed. Fiery Irishman Andrew Jackson Higgins was a visionary. Designing boats is an unusual dream for a landlocked Nebraskan, so this native Columbus resident moved south to New Orleans. His company, Higgins Industries, would focus on shipbuilding. Higgins's design and production of naval combat motorboats changed the course of World War II. General Eisenhower claimed that the Higgins boats

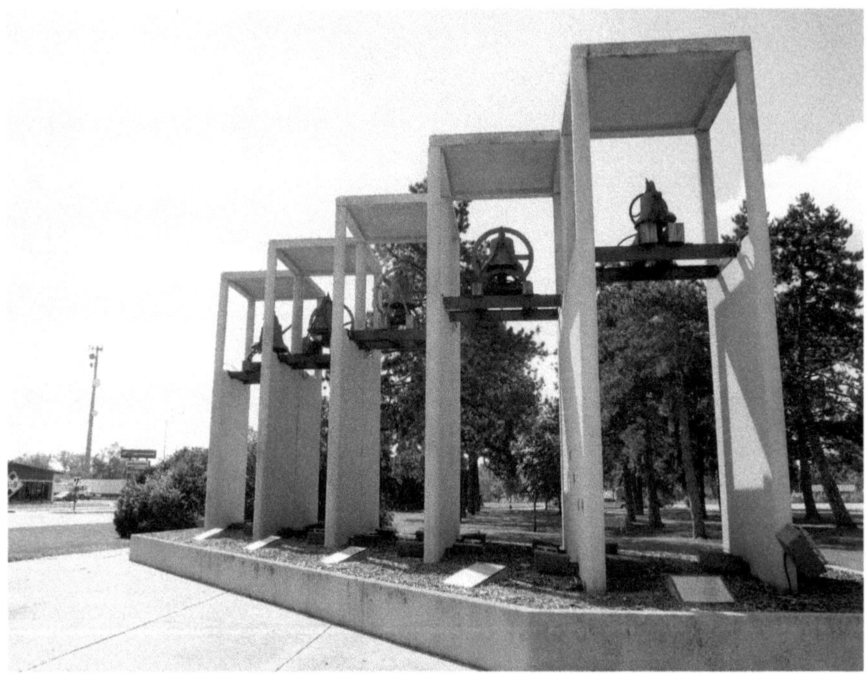

The Columbus Quincentenary Bell Tower displays ten former church bells.

were crucial to victory. Without Higgins's designs, soldiers would not have been able to land on the Normandy beaches.

The Columbus memorial honors both Higgins and history. Visitors can walk into a reproduction boat. Embedded in the surrounding concrete is sand from D-day beaches. Besides World War II landings, sand from Korea and Vietnam landings is also included. Constructed from salvaged World Trade Center steel, the 9/11 memorial statue pays tribute to freedom.

Across town, the Platte County Museum displays more sand samples from conflicts as well as additional artifacts. The Higgins Room answers other questions about both the man and his mission. While the park exhibit is free, admission is charged for the museum.

Merrick County

Wright Morris is recognized as one of America's most talented writers and photographers. He grew up in Central City, and his boyhood home can be toured by appointment. Founded in his honor, the Lone Tree Society schedules periodic area events to preserve his literary heritage.

Nance County

In 1879, Nebraska governor Albinus Nance approved this county. Despite the fact that the town was barely staked out, Fullerton became the county seat. Named for early settler Randall Fuller, this motivated man convinced Nebraska Wesleyan to move to Fullerton from Osceola. Despite Fuller's efforts, the university soon moved to Lincoln to be closer to more people.

The county museum is inside a historic Fullerton church building. On site is a former one-room schoolhouse as well. At a town park, the Nance County Veterans' Memorial honors area servicemen and women. A military resource center is available for those who need support.

Genoa's Varied History

Near the Nance County section of the Loup River passed part of Brigham Young's Mormon trail. For the first decade, these religious pioneers used wagon trains. In 1857, the demand for passage was too high. Then hand carts became the mode of travel. To assist travelers, way stations were built along the route. One hundred miles past their Florence winter quarters, Mormons established the town of Genoa. In a field near town, a marker notes the location where trail traces are still visible. After two years, this stopping point was no longer needed. The Mormons moved on, and the Pawnee Indian Agency moved in.

Although the Mormons are credited with founding Genoa, the Pawnee were there long before. Archaeological finds confirm the presence of Skidi and other Pawnee tribes. From at least the 1600s through the 1870s, Pawnee lived in large earth lodge villages. During annual summer and winter hunts, the tribe traveled and utilized tipis. Every spring, they returned to plant maize, beans, squash and sunflowers. Each fall, they came back for harvest. In 1857, life changed. A treaty required tribes to move to the designated Nebraska Territory Pawnee Reservation. One Pawnee village remained near Genoa, and four Pawnee tribes lived together. To teach reading and writing, a government school for Pawnee began in Genoa. In 1874, these Pawnee were forced to move to an Oklahoma reservation. For the next decade, squatters took over the schoolhouse.

Then the U.S. government decided to teach Native Americans the white man's ways. To enforce adaptation, Indian children were removed from their homes. In central locations, boarding schools opened. This former Pawnee agency was one ideal spot. From 1884 to 1934, the U.S. Indian School at Genoa hosted students from forty tribes. At its peak, almost six hundred students were at the school. The 640 acres contained thirty buildings, making this Nebraska location one of the largest federal boarding schools across the country.

To become a part of white society, students learned trades to enable them to make a living. Half days were spent learning reading, writing and math. During the remaining time, industry was the focus. For the boys, acquired skills were harness making, carpentry, shoe repair and tailoring. Nursing, cooking and sewing were the girls' trades.

Integration was expected. Students were not allowed to speak their native tongues or observe traditional customs. At first, this must have been troublesome. Tribes that once warred against one another were now expected to learn together. Over time, some benefits of this approach became apparent. Many students from different nations became friends. Native Americans learned to work together for the common good.

Today, part of the grounds are open for exploration. On the intact brick stile marker, designs and dates carved by the students engrave the bricks. Nearby are the railroad tracks that brought many students to school. Although the powerhouse is gone, the tall steam smokestack used to heat the buildings still stands. A memorial commemorates those students who died due to illness. In the confined living quarters, lack of immunity to disease became a problem.

At the onsite research center, Native Americans can find their connection to the school. Because the school was seen as a punishment by many tribes, the boarding experience was hard for students. For the families of former students, visiting has been a healing experience.

At the site of the former Indian school, the Manual Training Building is now the Indian School Interpretive Center. The campus scale model tells of the learning that once happened. Representing all the students' former Indian nations is a forty-flag display. Exhibits expound on boarding school life. Upstairs, the boys painted the walls with bridled horses and haltered cattle. Once visual teaching textbooks, now the murals are preserved works of art. Still on site is the former *Indian News* printing press.

Throughout the summer, visitors can take tours. On the second Saturday in August, annual events celebrate the school's heritage. More sections of the grounds, such as the now privately owned barn, are open to visitors then. During the off-season, visitors can make appointments to tour. Donations allow this important cultural museum to stay open.

Down the road in the former town bank building, the Genoa Historical Museum highlights both Mormons and Pawnees. Relics found within five miles of town compose the Allen B. Atkins Pawnee Indian Artifact Collection. At the town cemetery, a stone marker stands tall. Here remains from over eight hundred Pawnee were re-interred in the 1990s. Genoa's title of the Pawnee Capital of Nebraska is well deserved.

Northeast Nebraska Prairie Plains Properties

Finding several ecosystems in 112 acres of land is rare. At the site of the former Olson ranch near Albion, such landscape diversity exists. On the eastern edge of the Sandhills, the Olson Nature Preserve includes wetlands, prairie and a cottonwood grove. A steep north–south escarpment features an oak forest. The spring-fed Beaver Creek runs through the property.

In Colfax County north of Schuyler is the Frank L. and Lillian Pokorny Memorial Prairie. This forty-acre preserve includes a beautiful twenty-acre virgin tall-grass prairie, which is rare in eastern Nebraska. Twenty additional acres show the results of a very successful prairie restoration. These Nebraska Prairie Plains properties can be enjoyed by visitors who follow the exploratory guidelines.

NEIHARDT CENTER IN BANCROFT

In northern Nebraska I grew up at the edge of the retreating frontier, and became intimately associated with the Omaha Indians, a Siouan people, when many of the old "long-hairs" among them still remembered vividly the time that meant so much to me.

—John Neihardt's introduction to Cycle of the West

Although John G. Neihardt started life in other midwestern states, a move changed his life. At the age of eleven, Neihardt and his family settled in Wayne. This relocation changed the trajectory of his life. Soon after, he began writing the poetry that he would later be known for. After his Wayne Normal School graduation, he had a short stint as a country schoolteacher.

Then Neihardt moved to Bancroft, where he began to write professionally as well as edit the local *Bancroft Blade*. During this season, he also was a clerk for a trader for the Omaha Indian tribe. This interaction with Native Americans started his fascination with the local tribes. Neihardt wanted to give this long-silent culture a voice. His best-known book, *Black Elk Speaks*, is about an Oglala holy man.

At the John G. Neihardt Historical Site in Bancroft, visitors can glimpse the life of one of Nebraska's most prolific poets. A memorial room chronicles Neihardt's life and writing journey. Displayed memorabilia includes objects presented to Neihardt by Black Elk himself. Featured in the center of the museum building is a *cyad*, an ancient plant form that represents the tree of life.

Scholars may choose to spend time studying in the library. Although not a circulation center, visitors can make arrangements to view the available

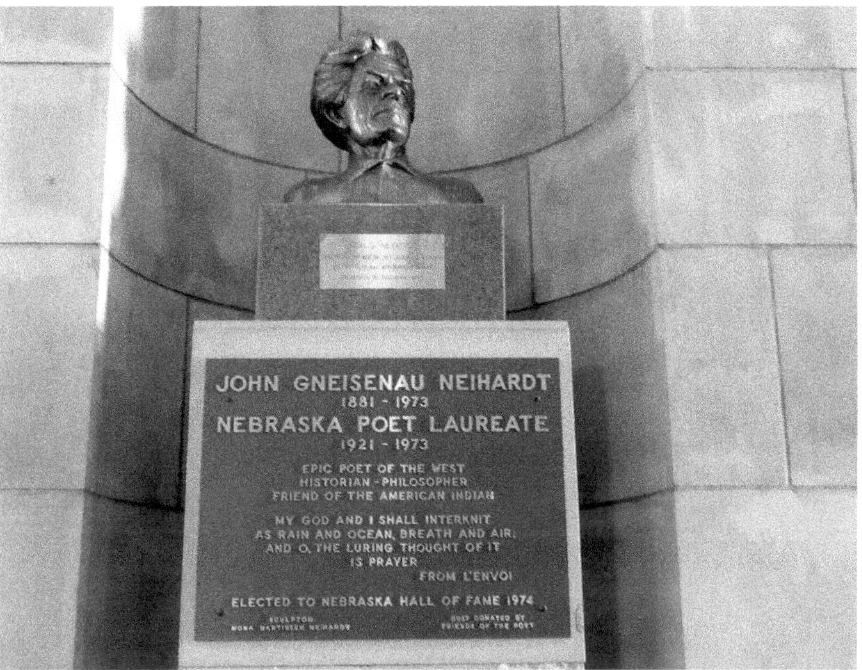

Poet John G. Neihardt is one of twenty-five individuals in Nebraska's Hall of Fame. Statues are displayed at the Nebraska Capitol.

resources. All the materials relate directly to Neihardt and the study of the West. Administrators continue to preserve Neihardt's heritage. Research assistance is a part of that process.

Only one building remains from Neihardt's initial twenty years in Bancroft. A small one-room shed was rented by Neihardt from 1911 to 1920 as his studio. Restored by the townspeople, this shed was where Neihardt composed some of his poetry and wrote part of his book *The Cycle of the West*. During nicer weather days, the open door allows guests an expansive view of Neihardt's writing room. Even if the door is closed, large windows allow visitors to peer inside.

Beyond the life of Neihardt, a better understanding of Native American culture and traditions can occur at this site. The Sacred Hoop Garden brings to life the author's experiences with Black Elk. Divided into four sections, each directional quartered section has a designated symbol, power and color. Designed by Neihardt himself, this outdoor area captures his heart. His dream was to represent nature and the plight of people through poetry.

Winnebago

The Winnebago people are survivors. From their early beginnings, war, disease and other hardships plagued the people. Displaced from neighboring states, this tribe settled in Nebraska. Today, this group is finding ways to thrive on the reservation.

At the heart of the Winnebago tribe is their commitment to keeping the Native American culture alive. Over two decades ago, the tribe started the Little Priest Tribal College. With a unique approach to higher education, students can earn an associate's degree. In addition to business and education, cultural degrees are a part of the curriculum. Scholars can take classes in Native American studies and learn aspects of indigenous science.

The Angel DeCora Memorial Museum and Research Center is located on the college campus. Exhibits emphasize the area's rich cultural heritage. Besides giving information about the tribe, this museum showcases the beauty of the land. The interaction between the American Indians and the European settlers is examined. Starting here provides visitors with a basic understanding of the Winnebago people. By seeing paintings of past and present leaders, visitors will see the relevance of this tribe today.

At the center of the Ho-Chunk Village area, Native Americans remember their roots. Lining the central circle drive is the Honoring-the-Clans Sculpture Garden. Representing each Winnebago clan are twelve concrete composite statues. Created by Winnebago native Charles Aldrich, the molded figures stand strong. Visualizing the role that each clan offers to the Winnebago tribe is possible now.

Norfolk Elkhorn Valley Museum

Back in 1958, a group of northeast Nebraska citizens formed the Elkhorn Valley Historical Society. Protecting the the heritage and legacy of these twenty-two connected counties was the mission. The members gathered stories and mementos to keep the area history alive. Almost forty years later, a beautiful building was constructed to display these memories.

What is unique about this museum is that the exhibits cater to multiple generations. Historical timelines recall notable locals, and early Elkhorn Valley artifacts are on display. Area residents can connect with the past.

In the Discovery Zone, children can experience educated play. Younger ones can make connections between the past and present day. For instance, the giant Lincoln log set relates to the actual log cabin found in the adjacent Verges Park.

In the agricultural area, a Square Turn Tractor commands attention. This Norfolk company manufactured machinery for several years before World War I. One of only three remaining tractors left, this agricultural machine is still operational. Other former farming tools are also featured.

One room pays tribute to one of the community's most famous residents. Although comedian Johnny Carson was born in Iowa, he considered Norfolk his home after he moved there as a child. Upon graduating from Norfolk High and the University of Nebraska–Lincoln, Carson joined the navy. Part of his service involved amusing the troops. When he returned home, he worked at Nebraska radio stations and entertained the locals with his magic act. To further his career, he relocated to California. On October 1, 1962, he started his career as a television host on *The Tonight Show*. He would hold this gig for fifty years.

Despite his fame, Carson did not forget about Nebraska. For the duration of his life, Carson often gave back to both the town and the state that he considered home. With Carson's input, the Johnny Carson gallery opened in 2002. While the display tells about his life, his *Tonight Show* years are the highlight. Clips, props and pictures provide a glimpse into the man behind the camera, and his six Emmy awards are also on display.

Neligh Mill

Enjoy chutes and ladders? Not only does Neligh Mill have plenty of those but also plenty of grinders and sifters. Steep stairs provide the avenue to explore all three floors. Crucial to Nebraska's early settlement, this location is an official state historic site.

As settlers were moving into Nebraska, a need arose for local flour production. Near the banks of the Elkhorn River, workers started construction. Right outside of Neligh, the flour mill opened in 1874.

Initially, stone burrs helped the grinding process, but modern steel rollers were soon added. This technology enhanced the flour's profile and elevated the mill's productivity. Besides serving the locals and other commercial locations, the mill had far-reaching contracts. Both the Indian Bureau and

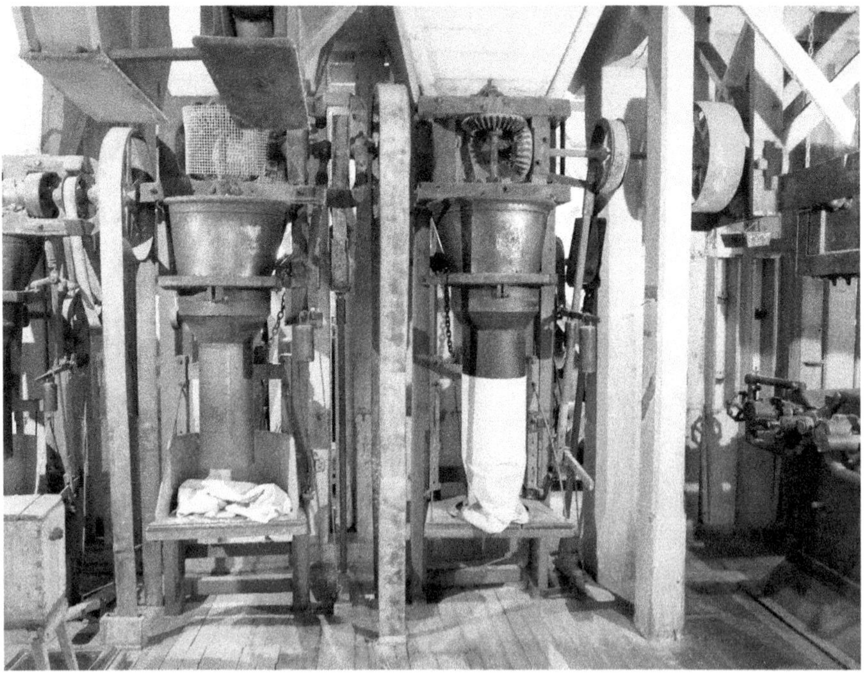

The Neligh Mill 1880s equipment is still intact.

the War Department sought out Neligh flour. At this point, England was even exporting flour from this site. Keeping up with the supply and demand was a challenge. As much as the river water level would allow, the mill was operational twenty-fours a day.

Even with an ownership change, Neligh Mill continued to improve in efficiency and productivity. For twenty-five years, this location also generated all of the town's electricity. During World War I, as the government needed more flour, consumer wheat flour was restricted. This resulted in corn being processed here. Even throughout the Great Depression and World War II, Neligh Mill kept up production. Once the second war was over, supply and demand slacked. Eventually, this location became a feed mill. In 1969, production ceased. The final owners wanted to preserve the mill. In part due to their own donations, their wishes came true.

Although numerous flour mills were once found across Nebraska, the Neligh Mill is the only intact nineteenth-century mill. Reconstruction of the flume and penstock, as well as the office building, was necessary. The main mill building and elevators are frozen in time.

OUTSIDE ROYAL

To supply the Grove Trout Rearing Station Fish Hatchery, personnel bring in four-inch fingerlings from the Calamus State Fish Hatchery. Upon arrival, the trout are fed and sorted. At about ten inches long, the year-old trout are relocated to Nebraska public lakes and streams. Although summer is the best time to visit the hatchery, limited tours happen year round. While there, visitors can pay a quarter to feed the fish.

Also outside of Royal is the Ashfall Fossil Beds State Historical Site. Other than at zoos, rhinoceroses and camels rarely roam in Nebraska. Yet these creatures are found buried here.

In 1971, University of Nebraska Museum paleontologist Michael Voorhies explored northern Nebraska. With his wife, Jane, he hiked the Verdigre Creek area. Wind and rain exposed the hilly landscape and provided the potential for fossil finds. At one point, Voorhies noticed a high sandstone cliff. In a nearby gully, a white bone jutted out.

Upon closer examination, he identified a baby rhinoceros's skull. Although rhino bones were in the area, an intact skull and jawbone were

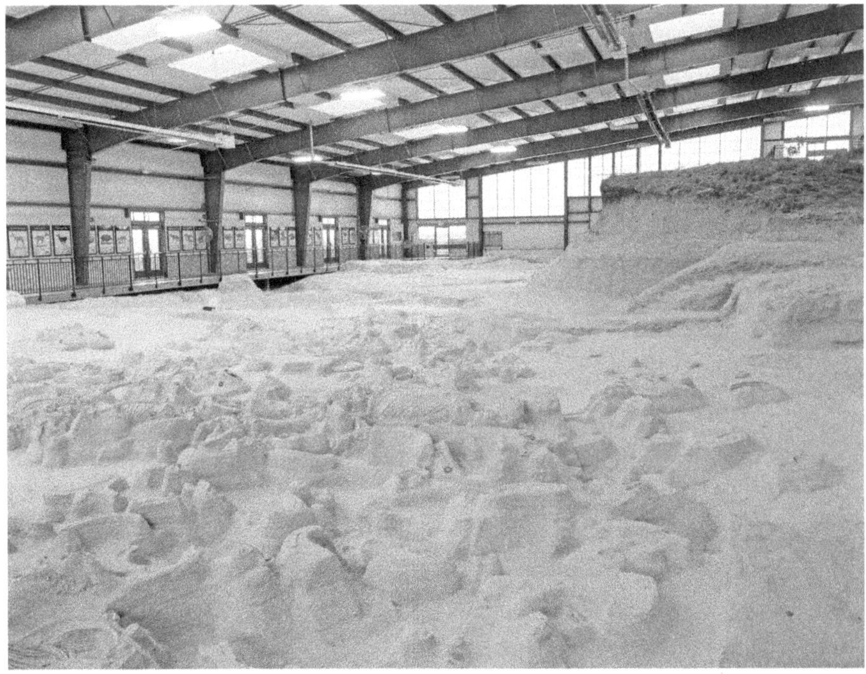

See an active dig at Ashfall Fossil Beds near Royal.

rare. Tempering his enthusiasm, Voorhies knew excavation was the next step. During the initial dig, five rhinos emerged—more than expected.

Several years later, Voorhies and his crew began unearthing skeletons. Abundant buried skeletons convinced *National Geographic* to sponsor an actual dig. Careful excavations uncovered more hidden bones. During the summers of 1978 and 1979, numerous finds astounded scientists. Complete skeletons of rhinoceroses, camels and horses appeared. Partial skeletons of deer, turtles and birds were also unearthed. The burial grounds seemed to continue far beyond the original dig site.

Scientists determined this location was an ancient watering hole. Because ash covered much of the site, they concluded an ancient volcano eruption determined the animals' fate. Comparing soil samples proved this ash spewed out in Idaho.

As the excavation area grew, the site became more accessible. In the summer of 1991, a state historical park allowed the public to observe these great finds. As time passed, the dig area kept enlarging as more fossil discoveries were identified.

Today, a large shed covers the fossil site. The walkway is mere feet away from the discoveries. During the summer, student paleontologists are on site, and visitors can actually watch fossils being revealed. Throughout the next decade, the Hubbard Rhino Barn area will be completely excavated. Nearby areas may also be uncovered. This location will preserve Nebraska's past long into the future.

Cedar County

When two British lords visited the United States in the 1870s, little did they know that they would forever leave a mark on northeast Nebraska. A railroad superintendent proposed that Coleridge and Hartington be renamed in these men's honor. Soon after, another Briton was honored. Randolph recognizes the contributions of English statesman Lord Randolph Churchill.

Outside Laurel, my father's hometown, is a memorial to World War II soldiers who died during a training exercise. My grandmother happened to witness the crash of the two B-17 airplanes from her kitchen window. Seventeen airmen from the Sioux City air base died when their two planes collided mid-air. Today, a monument along Highway 20 remembers these men's sacrifice for freedom.

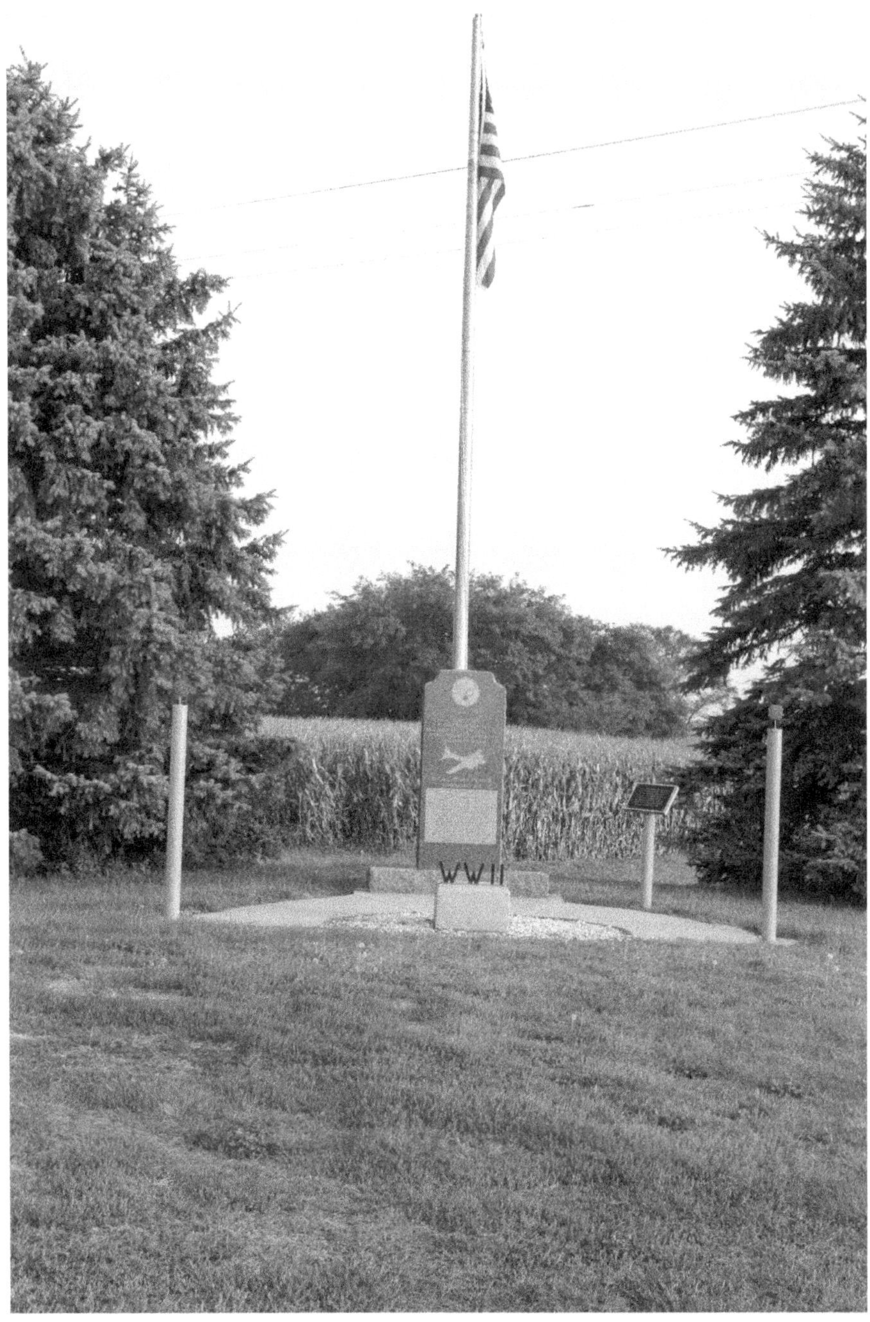

Near Laurel is this memorial to World War II soldiers who died during a training exercise.

LEWIS AND CLARK HISTORICAL TRAIL

On the northern edge of Nebraska, three popular locations are near the Lewis and Clark Historical Trail. Through the forested hills at Ponca State Park, visitors can explore the many trails. The wildlife is plentiful, and the Missouri River stretches far into the distance. At the Lewis and Clark State Recreation Area, a small interactive display tells about the intrepid explorers. Their 1804 expedition passed by the lake.

The Corps of Discovery Welcome Center is between Crofton and the South Dakota border. Nearby is a location where Lewis and Clark met with the Yankton Indians during their expedition. Inside, Lewis and Clark items are available at the gift shop. Area artisans consign wonderful handcrafted souvenirs. For travelers, available brochures tell about local businesses and area attractions. For the perfect travel break, hike the center's nature trails. Operated as a nonprofit organization, this location accepts donations. The organization hopes to welcome travelers long into the future.

NIOBRARA

An unsuccessful hunting trip changed Kenard Kreycik's direction. Rather than pursuing elk, he decided to raise them. Eventually, he added buffalo. Visitors would come from miles away to see his exotic animals. The Kreycik Elk and Buffalo Ranch tours began and became a family project.

To see the animals, visitors ride out in a covered wagon. Pulled by a tractor, this trailer allows guests closer access to the animals. Tamer ones can be hand fed. Tour guides tell about the joys and challenges of running the ranch. Exploring nearby beautiful Niobrara State Park is also recommended.

4
SANDHILLS REGION

With miles of grass, hills and wind covering over twenty thousand square miles, the Sandhills region is Nebraska's largest ecosystem. Not all of Nebraska's Sandhills acres are officially found in this subdivided region. Yet this particular section of Nebraska remains similar in landscape. Having traveled throughout this region, I can confirm that if you ever want to be alone, achieving that goal is certainly possible in this part of Nebraska. In fact, the state's nine smallest counties by population are found in this region. Several of these counties, including Arthur and Hooker, only have one incorporated town.

Because only sparse towns are scattered around, you do not want to enter this part of Nebraska without being prepared. Fill up the gas tank, because many, many miles will pass before the next station. Having a fully charged cellphone is also advisable. But recognize that cell service can be sparse in remote areas. After getting past this feeling of isolation, a kind of beauty rarely seen anyplace else inspires awe. The Sandhills could be its own destination. As only the hardy settle here, they bring to life the unique aspects of this region.

Valentine

Named in honor of Congressman Edward K. Valentine, this north-central Nebraska town was the last railroad stop for many years. To help

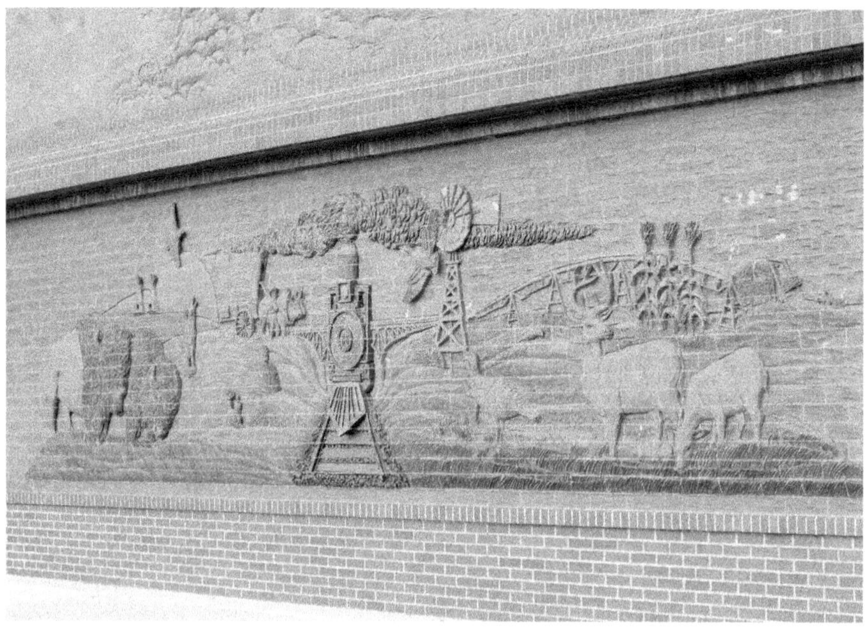

Jack Curan's mural on Valentine's First National Bank symbolizes early town growth.

Valentine be elected, his supporters resettled in this area. After the election, the community named the town for him. In the early days, thieves and other unsavory characters settled in this remote location. Today, Valentine is considered a part of the Outlaw Trail. Visitors can explore the known hangouts and hidden locations of men such as Doc Middleton.

Historical Museums

Two museums tell about Valentine's checkered past. Featured at the Cherry County Museum are the first white settlers, the cattlemen. Exhibits on Fort Niobrara, Native Americans and pioneers are waiting to be explored. This location has extensive research collections that include historic newspapers and genealogical records.

Centennial Hall is the oldest standing high school building in the state of Nebraska. Built in 1897, the building now serves as a remarkable museum. Area residents donated items, and the various rooms compel visitors to step into local history. The military room honors Cherry County veterans. The school room includes a collection of antique maps. In the cowboy room, the original wood slat jail leans against the wall. The Hallock Bells Collection displays 1,700 beautiful bells. Antique dishes, period furniture and vintage clothing are displayed. The trophy room keeps records of local school accomplishments and graduating classes. Since only one physician served the community for many years, the walls testify to his service. Dr. Farner's photograph collages document residents' childhoods. At this local museum, purposeful displays will intrigue even outsiders.

Both Cherry County museums are open limited hours from Memorial Day through early fall, but visitors can arrange their own appointments. Curators are proud to present their history. Minimal admission is charged at both locations.

Cherry County Area Water Life

For over a century, the Valentine Hatchery has raised fish. Using water from two area creeks, the process is completed using twenty-three stock ponds. Hatching warm-water fish, largemouth bass, blue gill and channel catfish are featured. Annually, the staff collects fish eggs from the regional waters. On the edge of the hatchery property is Government Canyon. This Wildlife Management Area is a great place for naturalists and outdoor enthusiasts to explore.

The Niobrara River

Valentine's proximity to the Niobrara River provides premium nature opportunities. The Nature Conservancy's Valley Preserve protects area trees, and nearby are two area wildlife refuges. At the Valentine National Wildlife Refuge, bird-watching opportunities abound. The Fort Niobrara National Wildlife Refuge hosts many local animals, such as prairie dogs. Driving through the refuge provides travelers a safe way to view potentially dangerous wildlife such as bison and elk. Water is also abundant. To view picturesque Fort Falls, the short hike down is steep. This path also leads down to the Niobrara River.

Smith Falls

Nearby is Smith Falls, Nebraska's breathtaking seventy-foot-high waterfalls. This stretch of land was first homesteaded by Frederic Smith. The next owner of the parcel, Fred Krzyzanowski, set up a basic campground for visitors to enjoy. Despite the remote location, many came to see this hidden wonder. Krzyzanowski encouraged exploration. Even in his later years, he walked from his home to visit with the campers.

Eventually, the Nebraska Game and Parks Commission took over and established a 250-acre state park. More visitors now enjoy this natural wonder. To provide easier access, a wooden bridge leads to the falls. With some assistance, even those with limited mobility can get close to Smith Falls.

Going down into the waterfall pool is even allowed, but the spring-fed water is rather frigid. Getting into the stream requires stepping on some slippery rocks. Climbing up might be even more challenging. This part of the adventure is not recommended for the solo traveler or for those who feel an aversion to getting wet.

The National Parks Service catalogued the waterfalls in Niobrara River area. To rangers' surprise, they found almost two hundred within a twenty-mile radius. Since most waterfalls are not on public land, access is limited to many. For instance, at times, the breathtaking Snake River Falls have not been open to the public. Now the largest Nebraska waterfall by volume can be enjoyed by visitors again for a small fee. Before trespassing, research first. Nebraska State Park areas are your best places to explore.

The Arthur Bowring Ranch

About an hour west of Valentine lies a tribute to Sandhill ranching. The Arthur Bowring Ranch is now owned by the State of Nebraska. Eve Bowring wanted to honor her husband's memory and continue on their cattle legacy. In 1894, Arthur established this Cherry County ranch, and Eve joined him there after their marriage in 1928. After Arthur's death in 1944, she continued running the ranch until her own death, another forty-one years later. In 1985, her foundation turned over the seven-thousand-plus-acre site to the state. The stipulation was that the location must remain a working ranch. Her prized brand of Hereford cattle still delights visitors.

Indoors, the family's unexpected collections will amaze visitors. Throughout the home, displays of antique china, crystal and silver collectibles

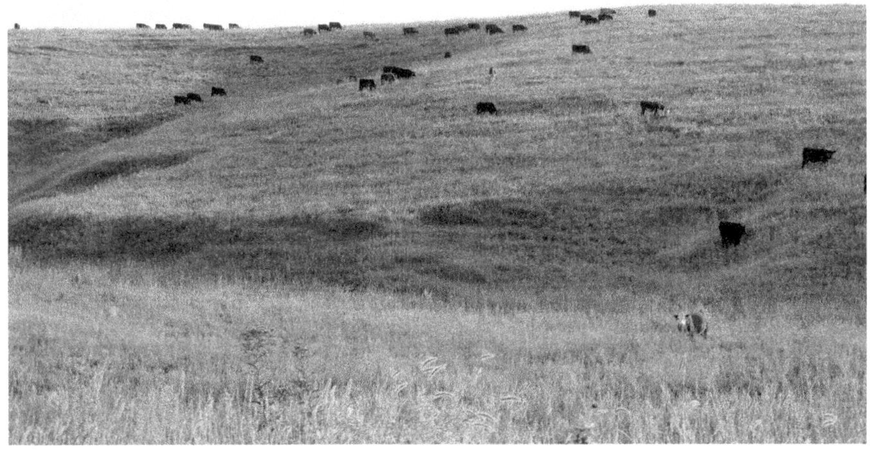

Grazing cattle are common in the Nebraska Sandhills.

fill shelves. Memorabilia from their political careers is also featured. Arthur was a county commissioner and a Nebraska legislator two different times. Eve was the first female U.S. senator appointed from Nebraska.

Besides featuring the Bowrings, the nearby visitor's center expounds on Sandhills history and geology. To further historical lessons, a replica sod house has been constructed on site. On the last Sunday in June, this park has Sodhouse Sunday. This event allows visitors to experience early Nebraska life firsthand. Typical pioneer activities are re-created, such as outdoor cooking and primitive crafting.

Nebraska's Least Populated Counties

Arthur County

The land now considered a part of Arthur County has switched hands a few times. First, Logan County claimed this portion. Then McPherson County had jurisdiction. Finally, in 1913, enough people lived in this section to claim independent county status. Yet this county is still Nebraska's smallest by population. In fact, at last report, Arthur County is the fifth-smallest county in the United States.

Arthur County has not let its size deter notoriety. From 1914 until 1962, Arthur County had the smallest operating courthouse in the country. Once court moved into a bigger building, this location became the county museum.

Arthur's Pilgrim Holiness Church is also noteworthy. Made with rye straw bales in 1928, this rare style of construction now is a community center.

Hooker County

This small Nebraska county only has one town, but little Mullen happens to be in an ideal location. The town is directly between two larger Nebraska towns: one hundred miles east of Alliance, one hundred miles west of Broken Bow. Being the only community in a sparsely populated region has its privileges. The Mullen public school system encompasses the whole county and beyond. Some Thomas and Cherry County students also attend Mullen's school.

A three-story building in town houses the Hooker County Historical Society. Tours are available by appointment. Near Mullen, visitors can drive by the historical Dry Valley Church. Services still happen there on Memorial Day and Christmas. Planning on staying overnight in Hooker County? The Sandhills Motel is your only option. The attached Glidden Canoe Rental allows visitors to navigate down the nearby Dismal River, a beautiful way to experience the Sandhills firsthand.

NEBRASKA NATIONAL FORESTS

Although many of the early surveyors considered the Great Plains to be a wasteland, pioneers would prove them wrong. This part of the country was misunderstood. Acres would soon become fertile ground, not only for agricultural purposes but also for trees. Both Nebraska national forests are in the Sandhills region.

How Nebraska has the largest hand-planted forest in the United States is primarily due to the efforts of one man. In 1890, Dr. Charles E. Bessey, a UNL professor, had a suggestion. He felt that growing trees would be beneficial for this wide-open area. Besides preventing erosion, trees would provide fuel and fence posts for the area ranchers. The test plots in Holt County were proven to be successful. In 1902, President Theodore Roosevelt declared two Nebraska sections were to be forest reserves.

Once named for the Dismal River, the first reserve encompassed ninety thousand acres. The Bessey Ranger District contains almost twenty-five thousand acres of hand-planted trees. Near Halsey, visitors can see the forest firsthand. In the Bessey Nursery, the trees continue to grow and thrive. The campground allows limited access to both the Middle Loup and Dismal Rivers. Visitors can drive the short distance to an observation tower. Although climbing the many stairs to the top requires a bit of effort, the views are spectacular. The lookout helps visitors to visualize the huge undertaking of the visionaries who planted all these trees.

The Samuel R. McKelvie National Forest might be a misnomer. This 116,000-acre area found in Cherry County is more of a tribute to wild prairie than to forestry. Mostly sprawling grasslands with occasional tree groves, 3,000 acres of trees do provide some stability to the land. Driving through this area is a highly recommended way to experience the raw beauty of the Sandhills.

THE VILLAGE OF TAYLOR

Farther northwest down Highway 11, drivers come upon the village of Taylor. This small town would blend in with all the others if an intervention had not occurred. Spearheaded by Marah Sandoz, the local community group wanted to stop the slow fade of its community. They wanted to go back to the time when the village was flourishing.

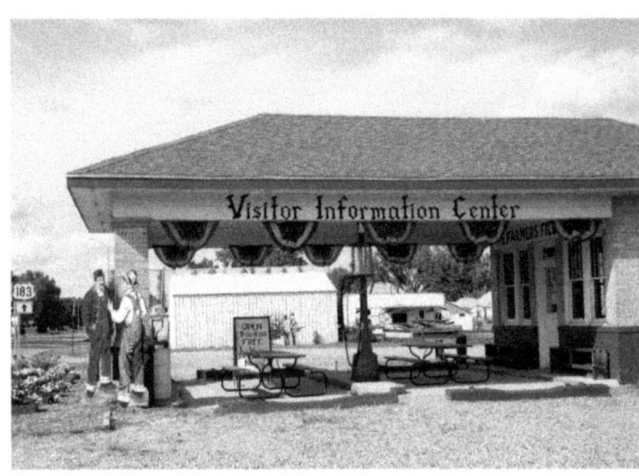

The villagers provide a historic welcome to Taylor.

Sandoz decided she would create life-size plywood reproductions featuring people from the past. From the 1890s to the 1920s, Taylor thrived. Her archival cutouts remind visitors of that time. Starting in 2003, historic villagers have started appearing around town. A few of the figures do represent actual residents. Most reflect the surroundings instead, such as the girl who appears to be chasing a butterfly through a small garden. The town population is increasing with the plywood characters. Over fifty historic villagers have "rejoined" the town thus far. These cutouts are putting Taylor on the map again.

CALAMUS FISH HATCHERY

Innovative procedures are happening at this northern Nebraska hatchery. To add oxygen to cold water, aeration towers are in place. Regulating the temperature happens with a heat exchange system. Featuring both wet and pathology labs, the staff provide fish with every opportunity to thrive. Several varieties of fish are at this location, but travelers should visit the water sources. The Calamus River and the Calamus Reservoirs are great recreational sites.

FORT HARTSUFF NEAR BURWELL

Less than thirty miles away, the location that guarded early settlers' safety is open again for visitors. Pioneers began to move into the eastern Sandhills area in the 1870s. Due to nearby Native American skirmishes, government protection was requested. Constructed in 1874, Fort Hartsuff was named for army hero George Lucas Hartsuff.

Besides providing protection to the newer area citizens, the soldiers were a visible presence of order. The nearby Pawnees also needed support against attacks from warring Sioux tribes. The force signified stability.

Evidently, the fort's establishment was enough to stop any trouble. Army men considered Fort Hartsuff uneventful and even boring; mindless maneuvers were endured daily. Once gold was discovered in the Black Hills, this lack of action caused a high desertion rate. The fort operated for only a short period of time. With the railroad's arrival in 1881, Fort Hartsuff was no longer needed.

During its short seven years of occupation, the fort did benefit the community. Both the soldiers and the local people were able to use the military hospital. Many of the early female settlers were provided work as laundresses. To stave off some of the inactivity, the men would also hold holiday balls. Performing plays and melodramas kept the soldiers active. The settlement became the social hub of this newly settled area, as homesick pioneers gravitated here. Once the fort closed, the settlers must have felt a sense of loss.

In 1961, Fort Hartsuff became a historical park, but restoring this post took time. All year, visitors can tour several former buildings. Still standing are the offices of the commanding officer, the quartermaster, the adjutant and the commissary. During the warmer months, a visitor's center and gift shop are also open. Sometimes Civil War reenactments and other living history events even take place at the fort. The goal is for visitors to be able to experience a bit of this pioneer past for themselves.

THE HAPPY JACK PEAK AND CHALK MINE

Up the road in nearby Scotia, travelers can explore a rare landform. The Happy Jack Peak and Chalk Mine is one of only two underground diatomite mines found in the United States. This central Nebraska site is the only one open to the public.

Before Nebraska was even a state, an army scout explored this cave. The explorer might have possibly been Jack Swearengen. Starting in 1872, this trapper guide and army scout was known to greet early settlers. The high hill and cave underneath were named Happy Jack Peak in honor of Swearengen. By the 1870s, the locals were mining the substance for building purposes. Soon they realized that this soft chalk-like substance had many applications. The silica-like material is found in paint filler, water filtration, fireproofing and concrete blends.

Although diatoms may resemble chalk, the composition is different. Diatoms are microscopic algae that are a one-celled food source for marine life. Visitors can see small fossils still embedded into some of the cave walls. In landlocked Nebraska, an underground area carved by water is unusual. Perhaps the location was the site of an ancient lake or was affected by a large flood. How long ago the cave was formed is a mystery, since no official records exist before the 1850s.

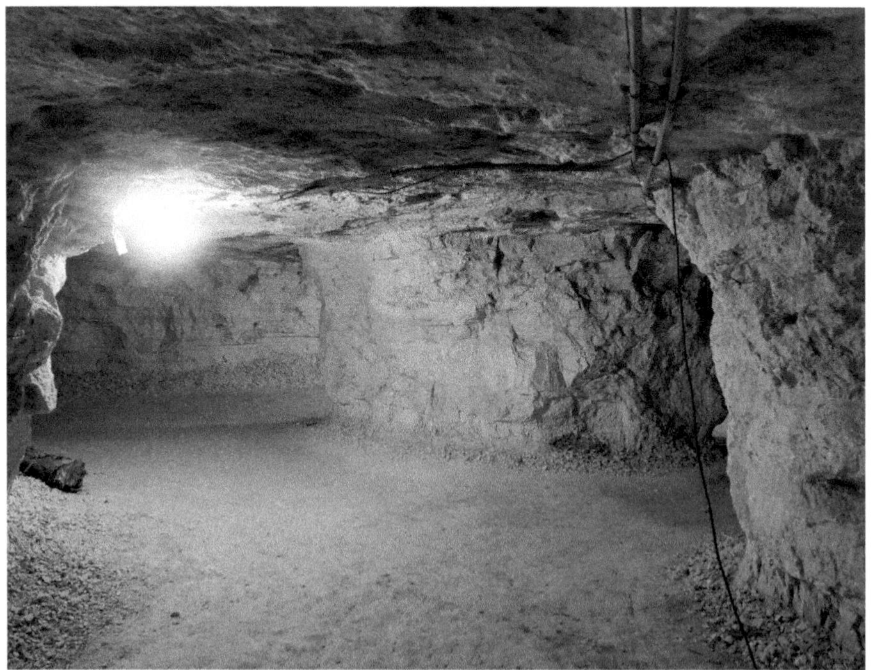

The Happy Jack Peak Chalk Mine is a cool place to explore during the summer, as the temperature is at least fifteen degrees cooler underground.

Due to safety concerns, only open diatomite mining is allowed today. After World War II, the Happy Jack Chalk Mine ceased underground mining. For a season, the mine was not accessible and remained undeveloped. Once lighting was added in 1997, the public could access this forgotten treasure again.

During the summer, when the cave is open for tours, traipsing through these trails provides a cool sanctuary. Temperatures drop at least fifteen degrees inside. Underneath the ground is six thousand square feet of caves. Only part is deemed safe enough to explore. What visitors can see is enough to tell the story of ancient history and the not-so-long-ago past. Besides being used for mining operations, this cave became a bit of a social hall. During the Great Depression, electricity was scarce. Cars would illumine the cavernous rooms to allow for evening dances. Through the years, the community has continued to use this underground location for gatherings.

ST. PAUL

The Museum of Nebraska Major League Baseball

The ball Gehrig hit was the same kind I fed him all through the 1926 World Series.... This time I gave him a screwball on the outside and look what he did to me. Goodnight!
—St. Paul baseball hero Grover Cleveland Alexander's remarks after Lou Gehrig hit a home run off of him in the 1928 World Series

On the edge of this Sandhills region, a museum pays tribute to a different avenue of Nebraska's past—the swinging kind. In the small town of St. Paul, on display are 140 men with Nebraska ties to the baseball big leagues. The Museum of Nebraska Major League Baseball was opened in 1999. But the story starts long before that—in 1887, to be precise. The first Nebraskan to be voted into the Baseball Hall of Fame was born that year in nearby Elba.

Grover Cleveland Alexander grew up on an area farm and graduated from St. Paul High School in 1909. Baseball was his game. His route to the Major Leagues involved several years playing semi-pro ball. A serious concussion almost ended his career before it started. This injury may have contributed to him suffering from epilepsy later on. Despite these setbacks, he debuted as a Philly in 1911.

By all accounts, Alexander was the best major-league pitcher from 1912 to 1920. Even today, he still holds the National League record for the most shutouts at ninety. Besides the Phillies, he would play for both the Cubs and the Cardinals.

In 1918, Alexander's baseball career was interrupted. Drafted to fight in World War I in 1918, this time spent away from the game would affect the rest of his life. Shrapnel in his arm, posttraumatic stress and the epilepsy would affect his ability to play ball. Even more devastating, Alexander chose to turn to alcohol to solve his problems.

Still Alexander managed to pitch for another decade and even had some brilliant moments. Striking out New York Yankee Lazzeri in the seventh inning of the seventh game of the 1926 World Series catapulted his team to the win. Over time, his alcoholism limited his reliability. During the last two decades of his life, he struggled both personally and financially. For his remaining years, Alexander found solace in his hometown of St. Paul.

In 1991, the town of St. Paul decided to highlight its native baseball hero. Grover Cleveland Alexander Days became an official annual celebration. In the following year, the town decided to honor Omaha pitcher Bob Gibson as well. Eventually, the St. Paul Chamber of Commerce decided to expand these displays into a museum. It expanded its vision to honor all Nebraskans associated with baseball's Major Leagues. Many community people put much time and effort into making this possible.

At this Museum of Nebraska Major League Baseball, the seven Nebraskans in the Baseball Hall of Fame have large displays in their honor. Besides Alexander and Gibson, Arthur "Dazzy" Vance, "Wahoo Sam" Crawford, "Richie" Ashburn, Billy Southworth and Wade Boggs are highlighted. Seven current major-league Nebraskans have larger exhibits as well. This lineup includes Alex Gordon. As left fielder, he was an integral part of the Kansas City Royals' World Series 2015 championship.

Picture plaques honor all 140-plus players who have Nebraska connections. A vast memorabilia collection includes baseball cards, literature, works of art and cartoons. These artifacts document Nebraskans' contributions to the sport of baseball. In 1952, Ronald Reagan portrayed Grover Cleveland Alexander in the movie *The Winning Team*. A special tribute to this film can also be seen.

Tubby's Firehouse

To tour another museum in St. Paul takes a bit of advanced planning. Tubby's Firehouse is often closed. In fact, the sign out front claims that the building only opens by chance or appointment. Because Ron Tubbs, an active Grand Island firefighter, owns and operates the museum, hours have to be limited. If the museum is closed, plenty of fire equipment is displayed outside.

The Sweet Shoppe

Down the street from both St. Paul museums, another icon is on display—the cookie jar. At last count, 1,620 jars are on display at the Sweet Shoppe. This stop is a perfect place to experience nostalgia. Enjoy a homemade treat before continuing on with your Sandhills exploration.

Broken Bow

In 1879, Broken Bow was founded. The name was suggested by two young explorers who found a pierced buffalo shoulder bone. A nearby broken three-foot arrow would decide the name of the town. During the town's early days, frequent conflicts happened between the cattlemen and the homesteaders. Perhaps all the brokenness did not only involve the buffalo. Today, this small town has moved past the bumpy start and is thriving.

At the edge of Broken Bow is the Sandhills Journey Scenic Byway Center. The Big Red Barn contains historical, archaeological, natural and cultural displays. Ranching and the railroad have affected this area the most. Nearby, the official Custer County Museum features the work of pioneer photographer Solomon Butcher. This man captured much of this region on film. Keeping local history alive is the mission of the dedicated staff and volunteers.

The Boneyard Creation Museum

Broken Bow is also home to another unique museum that studies the past. Geologist Steve Sommer started the Boneyard Creation Museum. The exhibits take a look at two opposing origin beliefs, creation and evolution. Themes include the Cambrian Explosion, the Mount St. Helens eruption and radioactive dating. Visitors can look over the origin evidence for themselves. Covering topics such as spontaneous generation, homologous structures and vestigial organs, this is not a lightweight museum.

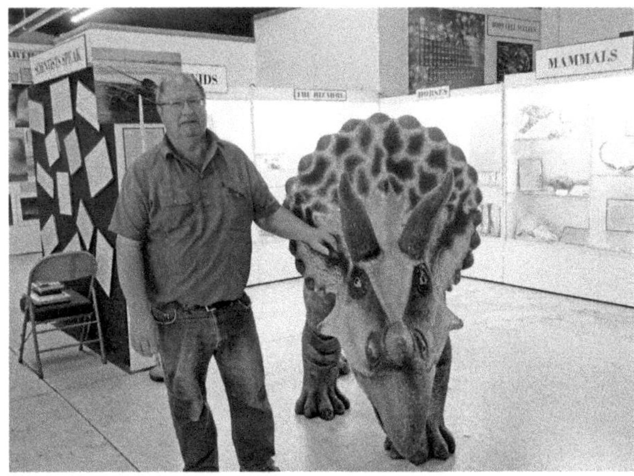

Geologist Steve Sommer, the Boneyard Creation Museum's founder, shows off one of his dinosaurs.

Even if some of the technical jargon is a bit much for a younger audience, kids will still enjoy visiting this one-of-a-kind location. Seeing replicas of big extinct dinosaurs and actual fossil remains will pique their interest. If this is not enough, being able to step inside a giant model of a human cell will definitely intrigue them. Understanding just how complex the human body is is fascinating for all ages.

Besides being a scientist, the owner is also a petrologist. His back room is full of rocks and gems available for purchase. Designing gem jewelry is also an option. Sommer hopes to start a new generation of rock hounds.

5
FRONTIER TRAILS

At one point, the central part of Nebraska was the country's final frontier. This unclaimed territory motivated both explorers and settlers to come. From the sandhill cranes to the pioneers, travelers along these trails are plentiful.

KEARNY, THE FORT

Frequently mentioned in pioneer folklore and fiction, Fort Kearny was a significant outpost. Named for General Stephen W. Kearny, this central Nebraska outpost came to be known as the "Guardian of the Plains." The proximity to the Platte River meant the Pony Express and Oregon, Mormon and California Trails passed by. The fort also helped establish relationships with Native Americans in the area.

This was not a typical fort. The original military site was ten miles by ten miles. Because the prairie was essentially wide open, the fort flagpole could be seen from the neighboring town of Lowell, eight miles away. While a wooden stockade was on site, the majority of the buildings were sod. Lumber was scarce on the plains.

Despite the many historical references in literature, Fort Kearny only operated from 1848 until 1871. In 1874, the fort was completely dismantled. Under the Homestead Act, the land was subdivided. The new owner had

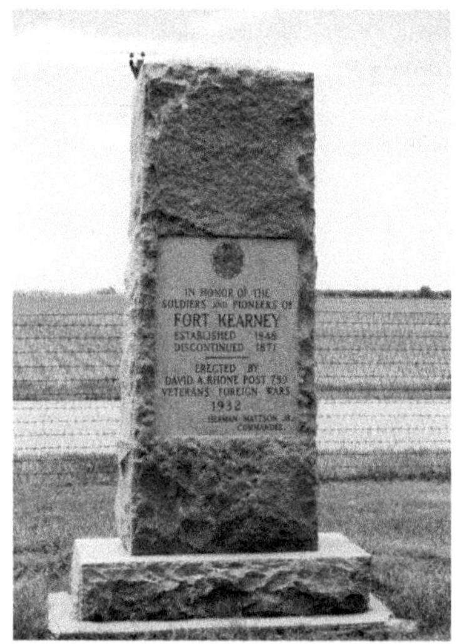

Fort Kearny was a key outpost for the pioneer trails.

the foresight to not farm the forty acres that housed the fort's original buildings and stockade. Although the land changed hands, the plow never touched that section.

In the early 1900s, efforts were started to preserve the site. In 1928, the Fort Kearny Memorial Association was formed. The original forty acres were repurchased and then donated for use as a Nebraska State Park. Restoring some of the structures and plotting out some of the original building sites took some time.

In 1959, the Fort Kearny State Historical and Bird Reserve opened. Over the next twenty years, the stockade and blacksmith shop were rebuilt. A visitor's center tells about the fort's purpose. Eventually, the completed powder magazine dugout area displayed historic ammunition. To visit, a Nebraska State Park permit is required.

KEARNEY, THE TOWN

Starting out as Kearney Junction, like the fort, the town of Kearney was named for Stephen W. Kearny. Unlike the fort, the town's name was misspelled. The post office added an "e" and then refused to remove the extra letter.

In 1873, there were 245 people living in Kearney. By 1890, over 10,000 residents called Kearney home. Hoping for even more expansion, locals invested in a cotton mill. The growth was invigorating. Certain their central location was better for the nation, residents petitioned to move the U.S. capital to Kearney. Their campaign might have been successful if not for the 1893 drought. By 1900, the mill had closed. Town population dropped by half, but the setbacks did not stop the area people. Kearney started to diversify. Once Interstate 80 went through Kearney, growth continued.

Today, Kearney calls itself the "Sandhill Crane Capital of the World." Considering 80 percent of the world's sandhill cranes migrate here annually, the name is justified. A public art project, *Cranes on Parade*, helped fiberglass birds stay on permanent display. Beyond these cranes, Kearney provides reasons for visitors to flock to town.

The Archway

The cowards never started. The weak died on the way. Only the strong arrived. They were the pioneers.
—from the plaque that greets Archway visitors

Stretching 310 miles, the Platte River crosses the state of Nebraska. Including tributaries, the waterway is even longer. The Archway celebrates the varied paths taken by travelers along this river roadway through the centuries. Retired governor Frank Morrison envisioned this museum educating travelers on the Platte's impact.

Normally, few attractions span an interstate. Especially not buildings weighing 1,500 tons. Constructing the Archway museum over I-80 required planning. Walking through almost two hundred years of U.S. history in such a short time span is rare. Experiencing this museum is an education.

To begin the journey, visitors climb the state's second-largest escalator. While wearing headphones, visitors can hear the stories of progress from a firsthand perspective. At several points across each room, different tales are told. Pacing is required. Listening well is necessary to catch all the details.

The stories start with pioneers. All three main western trails (Oregon, Mormon and California) passed nearby. The covered wagons came first. Thanks to sound and lighting effects, visitors experience a rainless prairie thunderstorm. The Mormon handcarts area conveys that not all westward travelers had the same experiences. Historical diaries are turned into first-person testimonies. On display is the tragedy and triumph of the 49ers. One corner exhibit seems like a junk pile. But that collection shows what travelers may have abandoned on the journey. Scattered furniture was commonplace.

Feet feel the thundering stampeding buffalo. Pictures on the wall change to show how fast the buffalo population disappeared. Before the white settlers, the Native Americans traveled the Platte Road. Exhibits convey the struggle between these two different ways of life.

At a gallop, the Pony Express rider appears. A message arrives via telegraph. Packed inside the stagecoach are many riders. Traveling under the train bridge demonstrates the danger of this new transportation mode. A figure representing Mark Twain stands near the stagecoach. Walking into these exhibits brings them to life.

Time transitions, and progress is made. Visitors climb into the next century. With the advent of the automobile, the Lincoln Highway provided one way for America to travel the country. Both a drive-in and diner mock-ups demonstrate changes made across the country. Through the glass windows, visitors can see the current I-80 traffic whizzing by underneath. The Platte River Roadway is still relevant. This fascinating approach to education is more than worth the cost of admission. Visitors should allow at least an hour to walk through the Archway.

This location is also a great rest stop. Outdoors, visitors can navigate through the Trailblaze Maze. Also on site are both earth lodge and sod house reproductions. A miniature silo and other shelters provide perfect picnic spots. On the grounds, statues and plaques tell of local history.

Nebraska Firefighter's Museum and Education Center

On the edge of Kearney is the Nebraska Firefighter's Museum. Three Nebraska firefighters wanted to create a museum to honor their fellow fighters for their service. Thirty years passed from the time of discussion to completion. Two were still alive to see their dream come true. After relocating the museum near the Archway in August 2009, development has continued.

Thanks to a vast collection, displays change frequently. Artifacts and even fire trucks show the history of firefighting from past to present. Visitors learn about Nebraskans' role in fighting fires. Exhibits explain fire prevention and show new firefighting developments. Kids love playing in the small fire engine and seeing the even smaller collectible fire trucks.

Community involvement is encouraged. Besides field trips, groups gather for celebrations that include birthday parties. Open year round, the admission charge goes for upkeep. Outside, the Nebraska Firefighters and EMS Memorial is free for all to enjoy during daylight hours.

MUSEUM OF NEBRASKA ART (MONA)

Housed in a beautiful Neoclassical 1911 building, MONA captures Nebraska's essence. In 1976, the museum started small. At that time, the Nebraska Art Collection Board only owned thirty pieces. Yet these board members were determined. Once the Nebraska legislature designated this artwork as the official state collection, donations increased. Forty years later, the museum has amassed over six thousand works of art. Most pieces can be seen online.

All eleven galleries rotate displays throughout the year, with current exhibits listed on the museum's website Sometimes particular artists are highlighted. Other exhibits involve a theme such as fiber or photography. One display featured sandhill crane art.

An artist's entrance into MONA's collections is discretionary. Five criteria are set. Preferably artists are born or have lived in Nebraska, but being trained or having worked in Nebraska is also permissible. According to MONA's website, "artworks that reflect the culture of Nebraska" are occasionally acceptable.

Beyond the galleries, MONA's collections influence the whole state. For a fee, the Artreach program helps Nebraska organizations fill galleries. Specific MONA pieces supplement locational displays. Promotional educational resources are provided.

Being associated with the University of Nebraska–Kearney campus complements MONA's value of education. A variety of classes are offered to all ages, as are guided tours and field trips. Advance Learning Days include studio art experiences and optional writing activities. Through videos on the museum's Nebraska Artists' website, connections are made to current state artists. Also online are actual art lessons.

CLASSIC CAR COLLECTION

To say Bernie Taulborg likes cars is an understatement. At first, his interest ran toward Cadillacs. Eventually, he searched for Buicks. To add to his collection, Taulborg scoured the *Hemmings Motor Magazine*. Often the glossy pictures compelled him to buy cars without looking them over first. Sometimes, he would travel to distant locations to make purchases. His automobile holdings grew. In 2011, Bernie and his wife, Janice, donated their 131 cars to start Kearney's Classic Car Collection.

Now the museum contains over two hundred cars. From an 1877 Selden replica to a 2001 Chrysler Prowler, all cars are in mint condition. Three Rolls-Royce models are featured, including a 1938 limo. A rare 1967 Rover Sedan is also here.

Displays add interest to the collection. The re-created 1950s gas station is complete with technician tools. At the drive-in movie theater area, local memorabilia is shown. Historical footage demonstrates the auto industry's beginnings. Some of these films are not shown on screens. Instead, re-created car hoods display the movies. Admission helps this museum stay open year round.

Pearl Harbor Survivors Preserve North of Kearney

The central Nebraska loess hills feature rolling plains of short-grass prairie. This Prairie Plains 320-acre property was donated by Pearl Harbor survivor Howard Juhl. His gift honors his fellow servicemen. Due to uneven terrain at this location, hikers need to tread carefully.

Minden

In 1891, the Minden Opera House brought culture to town. Even in smaller Nebraska towns, the second floors of retail buildings were for entertainment. Besides musical offerings, the large rooms held theatrical acts and gatherings such as dances. This Minden location became the town social hall. Later, with the advent of movies and other entertainment options, performances came to a halt in the mid-1950s. The building gradually fell into disrepair.

Decades later, the town decided the building was worth restoring. Through community support, area volunteers and workmen repaired the opera house and made improvements. In the downstairs section, theater offices and a gift shop provide the support network for the building. Upstairs, an expansive mural helps visitors visualize the history of Kearney County.

On Memorial Day weekend in 2000, the Minden Opera House opened again for performances. A community theater troupe presents a few productions per year. Other local and national acts also perform. Upstairs in the backstage green room, acts sign the walls after performances. This re-formed building will be marking history in Minden long into the future.

PIONEER VILLAGE

In a mere hundred and twenty years of eternal time, man progressed from open hearth, grease lamps and ox carts to television, super sonic speed, and atomic power. We have endeavored to show you the actual development of this astounding progress as it was unfolded by our forefathers and by ourselves.
—Pioneer Village founder Harold Warp

As the twelfth child of Norwegian immigrants, Harold Warp grew up in Minden. From the start, he valued resourcefulness and always tried to determine the best way to go about doing things. As a young man, Warp thought that putting glass into chicken brooding houses was not cost effective. So he invented a new material: flex-o-glass. To start production, Warp would need to relocate.

In 1924, Chicago was the current center of the mail-order world. With patent and cash in hand, he started the Warp Bros. Flex-o-glass Company. Warp developed more inventions and became an early plastics pioneer. He introduced prototypes for both commercial garbage bags and plastic food wrap. Today, the Warp Bros. Company is still a plastic industry leader.

In the 1940s, Warp was drawn back to Minden. He heard that several historic area buildings were slated to be demolished. One was the schoolhouse he attended as a child. Warp purchased them all and then started Pioneer Village as a tribute to his parents.

Warp's fascination with technology determined the museum's focus. This location chronicles innovations from about 1830 to the modern day. Presenting how innovations affected American life motivated him. From kitchen plumbing to aeronautics, displays illustrate the chronological progress of technology.

With over fifty thousand items contained in twenty-eight buildings, Pioneer Village's collections are extensive. The main exhibit features inventions. Beyond Warp's childhood school, the created town has expanded. To name a few buildings, a Pony Express station and land office were added. Large sheds contain automobile and agricultural collections. Both a campground and motel allow visitors to stop and stay awhile. Two-day passes are available.

Grand Island

For its first forty-one years, the Nebraska State Fair rotated between four towns. Then, from 1901 to 2009, Lincoln hosted the state fair. At that point, the University of Nebraska's Innovation Campus took over the former fairgrounds. Although the fair's move to Grand Island was controversial, now many agree the new central Nebraska location is beneficial—especially in highlighting the agricultural component of the state.

During late August through Labor Day, the Nebraska State Fair takes place. Typical exhibits feature 4-H, animals, mini shows and concerts. Fair food and midway rides entertain.

The Nebraska Game and Park Outdoor Commission's permanent exhibit transports visitors to the Niobrara River Valley. Filled with Nebraska fish, the giant aquarium and waterfall pond show the importance of streams and rivers. Interested participants can take a shot at both the onsite archery range and shooting gallery. Other displays illustrate outdoor living.

One building at the fair is open year round. Raising Nebraska provides an interactive agricultural experience. In the agri-house, visitors see how farming affects everyday life. Through touchscreens, the curious learn about aquifers and soybean/corn production. A life-size irrigation pivot and open combine cab encourage exploration. The Walkable Map of Nebraska beckons guests to discover the state's varying terrain.

Outside, native plants and grasslands grow. Crops are cultivated. By fair time, cornstalks, bean rows and more plantings await. Volunteers explain about water management and pest control practices. Teaching about agriculture in a concentrated environment is beneficial.

Stuhr Museum of the Prairie Pioneer

About sixty years ago, the concept of establishing a Hall County museum came under consideration. Grand Island resident Leo Stuhr was so committed that he offered up his family farm as a location. Making his desire a reality took a bit of time and lots of effort. On July 30, 1967, the iconic Stuhr building opened. Throughout several decades, the museum continues to grow.

Inside the main building, displays explore the lives of the prairie pioneers. Rotating exhibits show off art and more historical themes. In the Kids

Corner, children can play with toys and historic games. Across the outdoor walkway is the Gus Fonner Memorial Rotunda. Fonner donated his collection of Native American and western memorabilia. An antique farm implement section displays an extensive amount of machinery. At the railroad exhibit, visitors get an up-close view of historic trains.

One highlight of the Stuhr Museum is Railroad Town. From May 1 through Labor Day, this re-created town comes to life. Throughout the town are living historians playing parts from over a century ago. Wearing period costumes, interpreters help visitors feel transported back in time. Around town, the exploration options seem endless. At the emporium, period items are sold. The millinery shop still creates hats. Authenticity is found at every turn.

Other early Nebraska houses are also represented at the Stuhr Museum. Visitors can see how Native Americans functioned in the reconstructed Pawnee earth lodge. Back in the day, lodges of similar size would have housed at least thirty people. With grazing buffaloes close by, the tipis show the life of a hunter. The nearby actual pioneer trail guided many west.

The eight-structure Road Ranche cabin settlement features two authentic cabins. Located along migrant trails, at these locations repairs could be made and provisions could be purchased. One building from the former large Taylor Ranch is now on site and can be viewed from outside.

HASTINGS MUSEUM

Amassing artifacts became Albert Brooking's obsession. But not just for his own satisfaction—Brooking wanted everyone to access his specimens. The Hastings Chamber of Commerce supported his mission, and the Hastings Museum started in 1927. After two schools provided temporary locations, the collection moved into its own building. Eventually, this location became the largest municipal museum between Chicago and Denver. Collections contained at this site are like ones found in those larger cities. Until his death in 1946, Brookings stayed on as director and devoted his attention to the museum. In actuality, his body never left. His crypt is in the museum basement.

Renowned sculptor Gary Staab got his start at this museum. As a Hastings College intern, Staab sculpted some of the creatures found in the Cretaceous Sea exhibit. His knack for creating is evident. Today, Staab's sculptures are found in museums around the world.

In addition to ancient creatures, current animals are a part of diorama displays. From cougars to caribou, animals are set in painted displays matching their natural habitats. Guests can walk around the twelve-foot polar bear. Plexiglas allows him to be seen at all angles. The serial bird collection is the largest display in Nebraska. Every bird that migrates through the state is included. Insects, rocks and fossils are also categorized.

This museum also includes American history. Lock, Stock and Barrel presents the history of firearms. Discover how culture developed and survived for all in People on the Plains—from the Native Americans to the pioneer. Antique vehicles illustrate transportation progress. Hastings also contributed to World War II. Outside of Hastings, the Naval Ammunition Depot supported the army in a literal way. This exhibit commemorates the depot's sixteen-year impact on the community.

Inventor Edwin Perkins first made Kool-Aid, Nebraska's state soft drink, in his Hastings-area shop. One can walk through Kool-Aid's history, and Perkins's life is also on display. My kids' favorite part is seeing the clips of the Kool-Aid commercials from various decades.

The newest exhibit to the museum is the Nature Nook. This room was developed in collaboration with agricultural groups and area teachers. Featuring a replicated tree tunnel and interactive stations, visiting children can explore nearby Nebraska habitats.

The recently updated planetarium teaches about astronomy and has various shows. Hastings is the smallest community in the world to have such a large format theater. Besides documentaries, some of the latest Hollywood films also appear on screen.

PRAIRIE LOFT CENTER FOR OUTDOOR AND AGRICULTURAL LEARNING

Ingleside needed a new purpose. This former farm was part of the now-closed state mental hospital. Once considered the best dairy around, animals from cows to pigs to ducks had roamed the grounds. Acres of cabbage and other plants filled the fields. The greenhouse plants even included bananas. Now the farm was empty.

In 2000, a local group decided to transform these rural buildings into an experiential educational site. Eight acres were eventually purchased. Over time, the structures were salvaged. Another area house and livestock barn

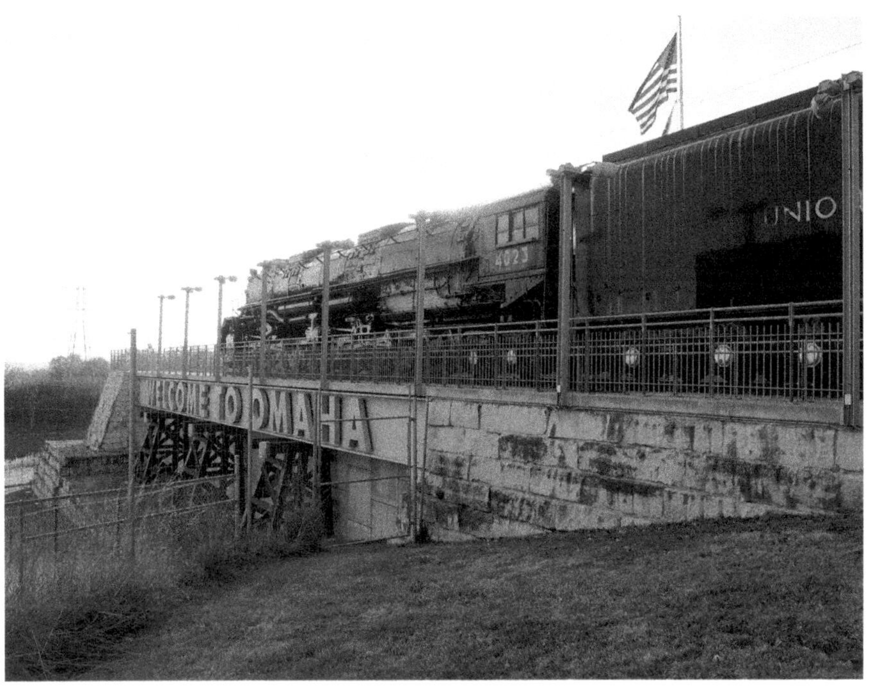

Omaha welcomes drivers coming in from Iowa on Interstate 80.

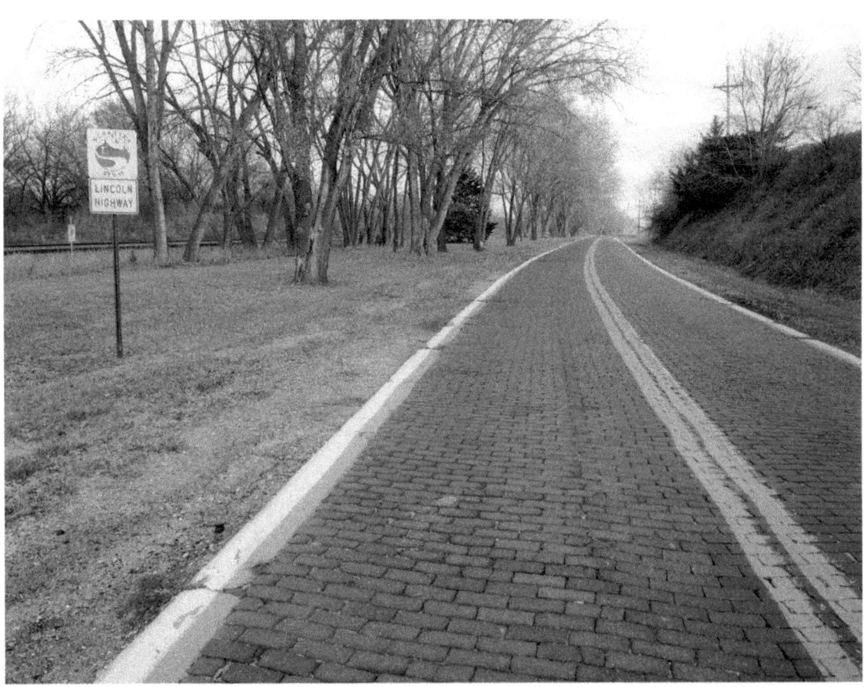

Bump along a stretch of original 1920s Lincoln Highway brick pavers near Elkhorn.

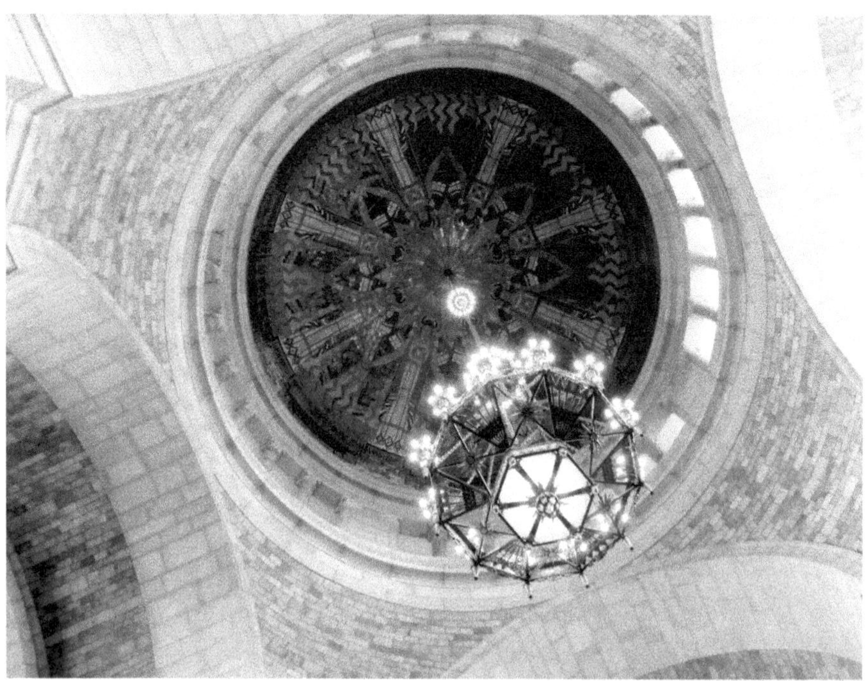

The third Nebraska Capitol's design symbolizes the state.

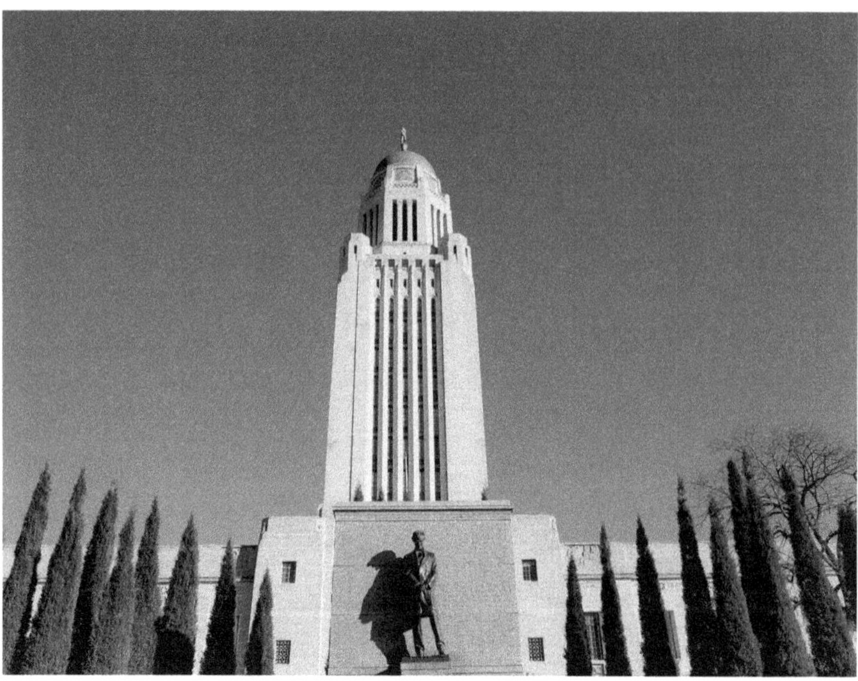

The Abraham Lincoln statue on the capitol's west side predates this building by over a decade.

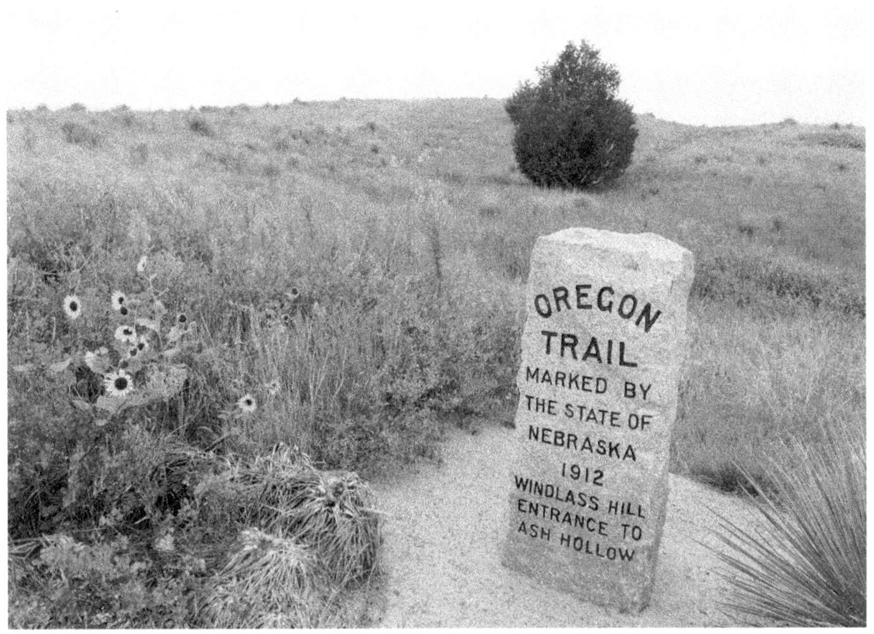

Climb Windlass Hill near Ash Hollow State Historical Park to experience a bit of the trek pioneers must have experienced crossing the plains long ago.

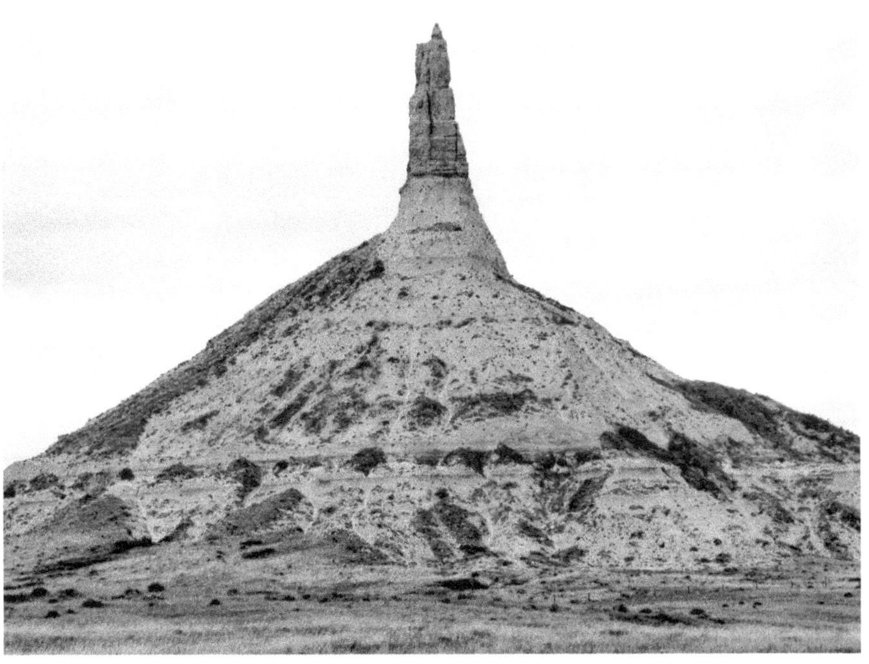

Chimney Rock is one of the most famous Oregon Trail landmarks.

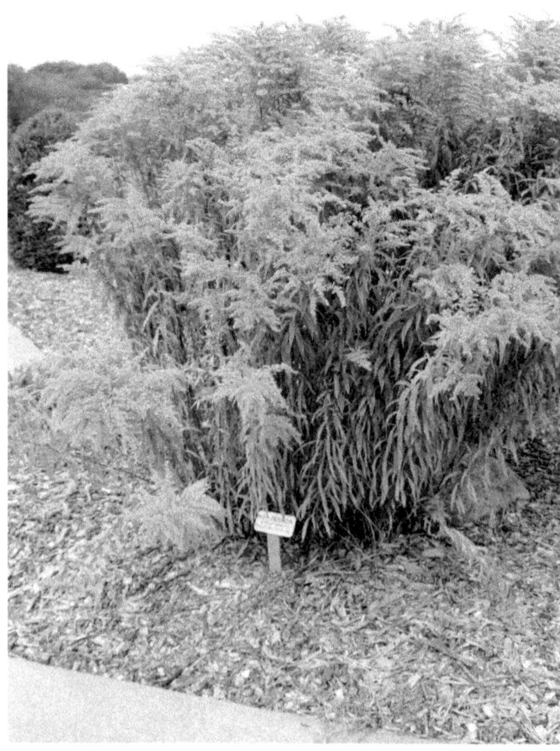

Left: Nebraska's state flower, the goldenrod, blooms in late summer and early fall.

Below: Apple trees at the Nebraska City Arbor Day Farm, where Arbor Day began.

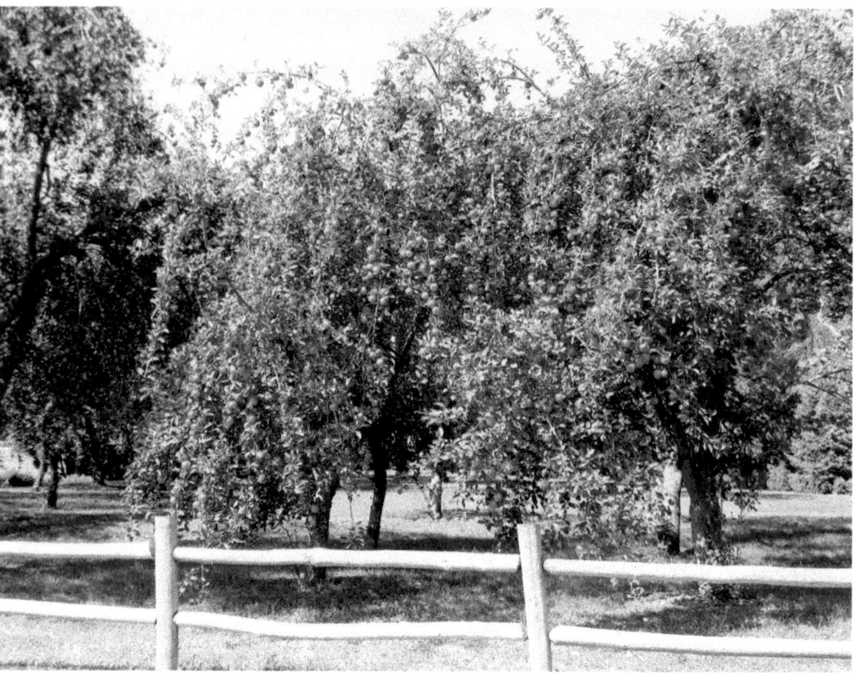

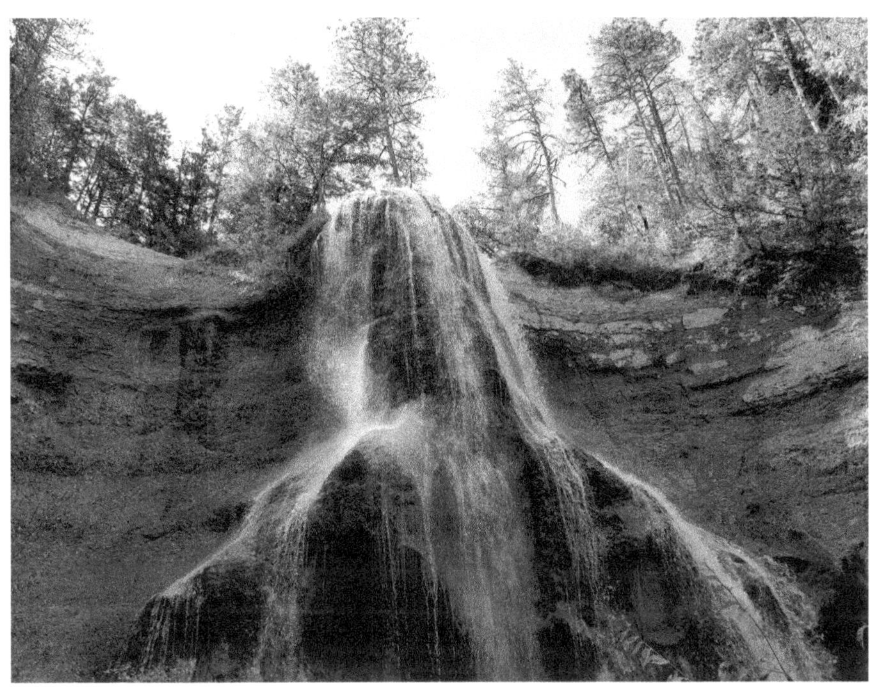

Smith Falls near Valentine is Nebraska's highest waterfall.

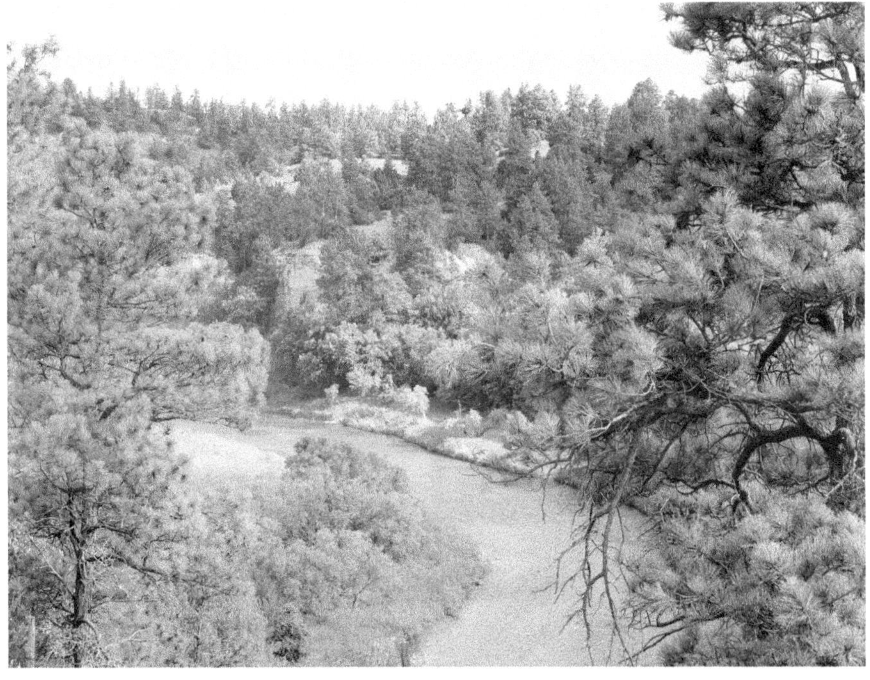

Niobrara, which means "flowing water," is considered an official national wild and scenic river.

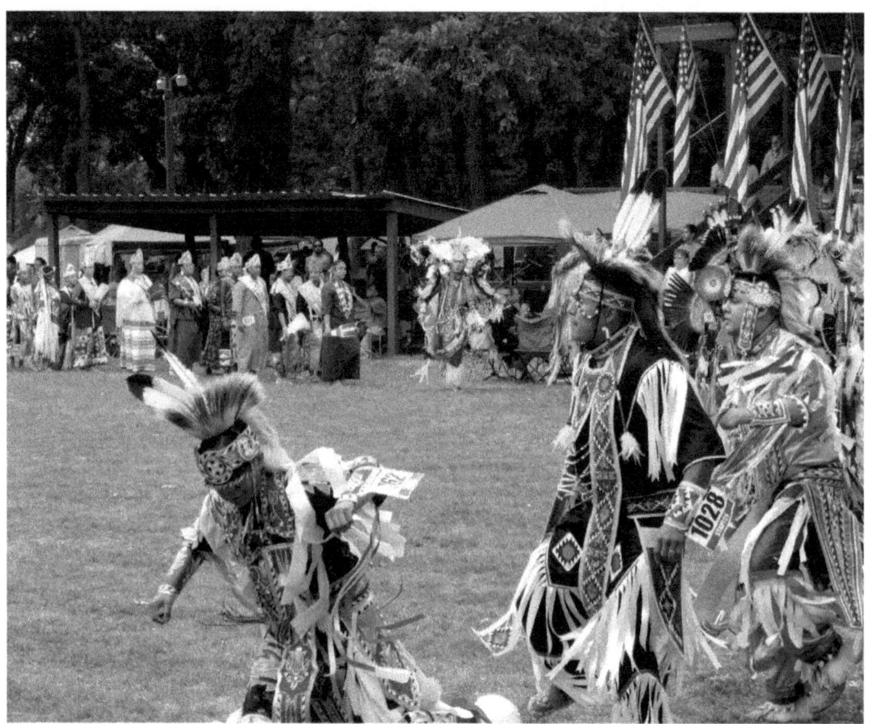

Members of the northeastern Nebraska Winnebago tribe celebrated their 150th annual powwow event in 2016. *Photo by Tim Trudell.*

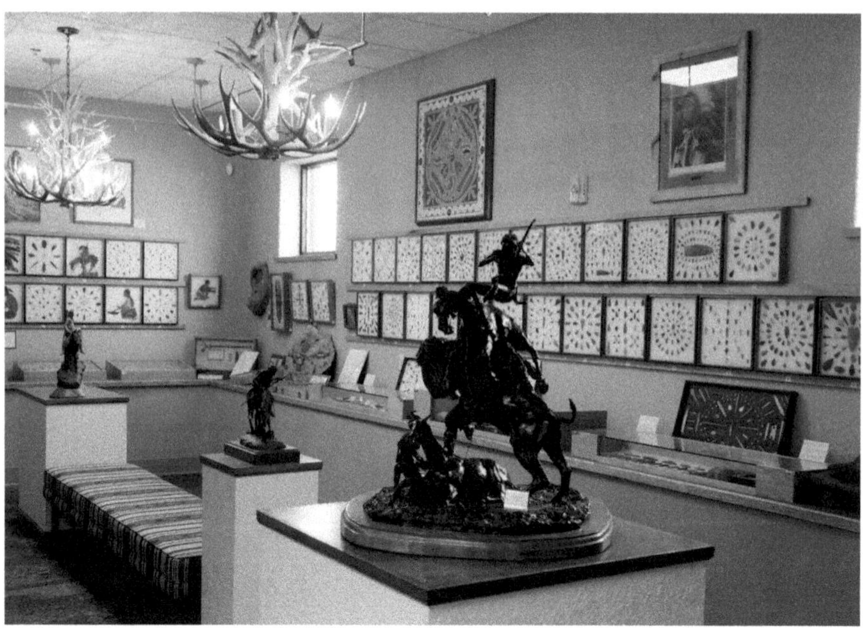

The Petrified Wood Gallery in Ogallala features western art.

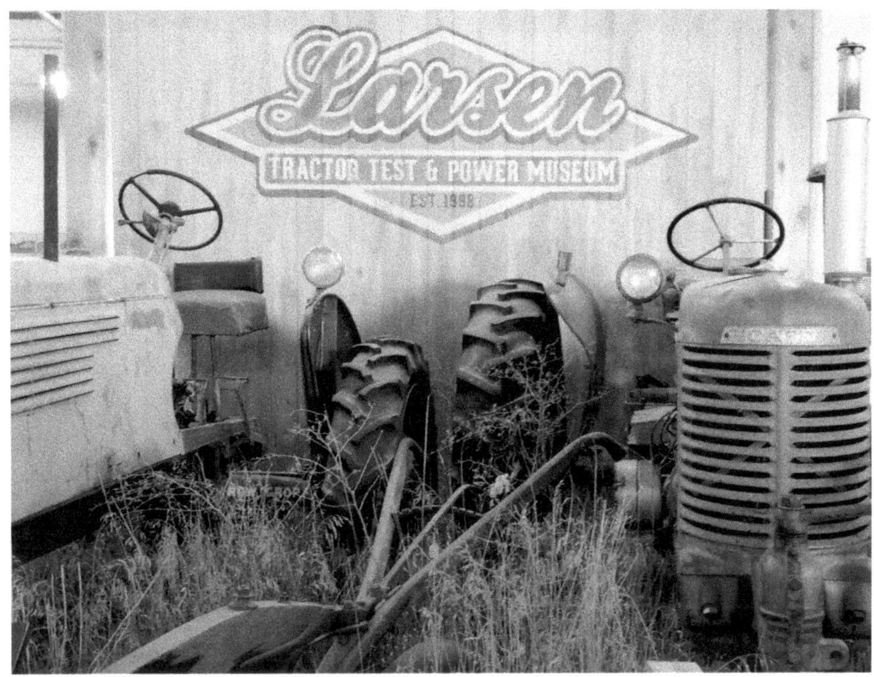

University of Nebraska–Lincoln's East Campus has the world's only tractor test lab.

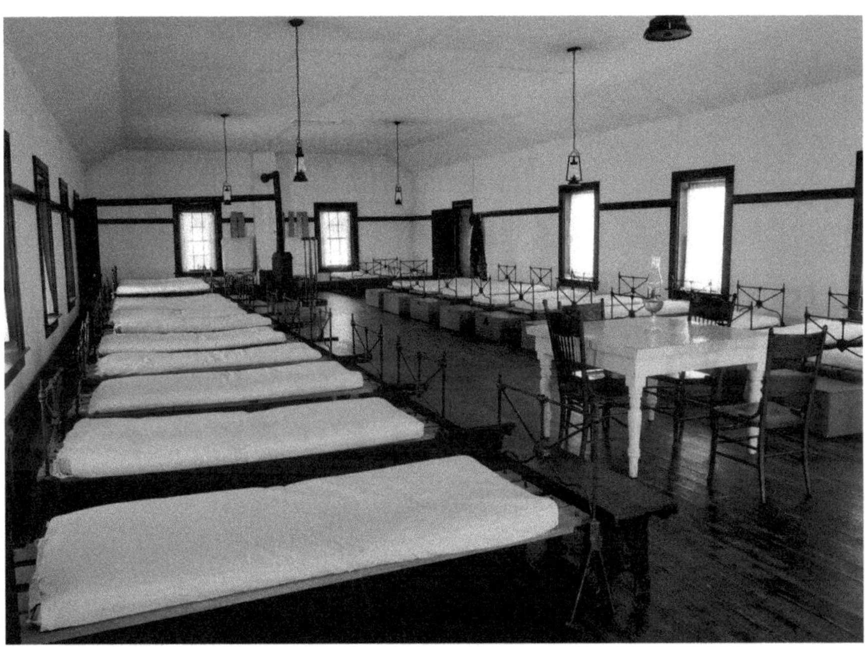

Fort Hartsuff's original enlisted men's barracks.

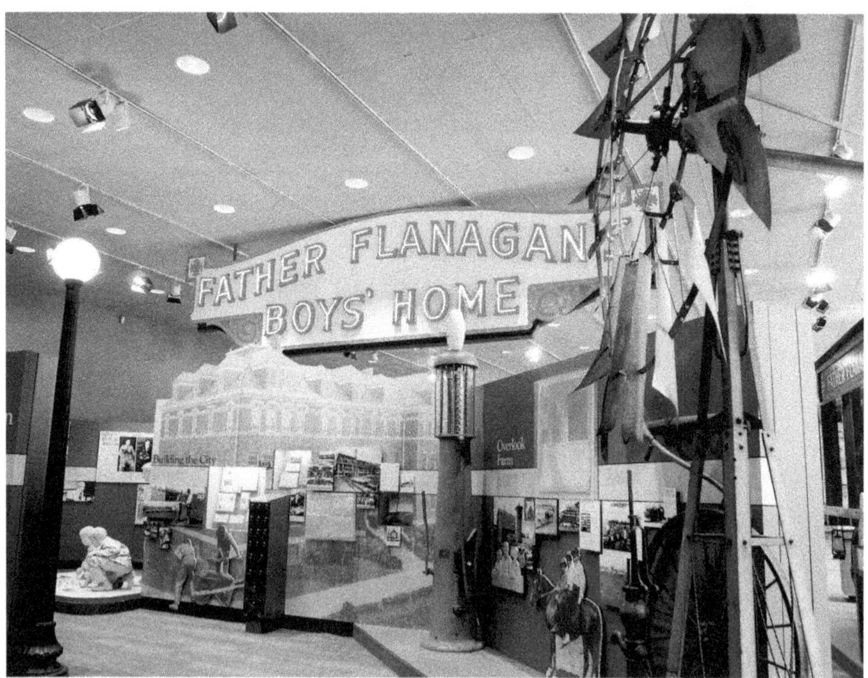

Learn more about Father Flanagan's humanitarian efforts at the Boys Town Hall of History.

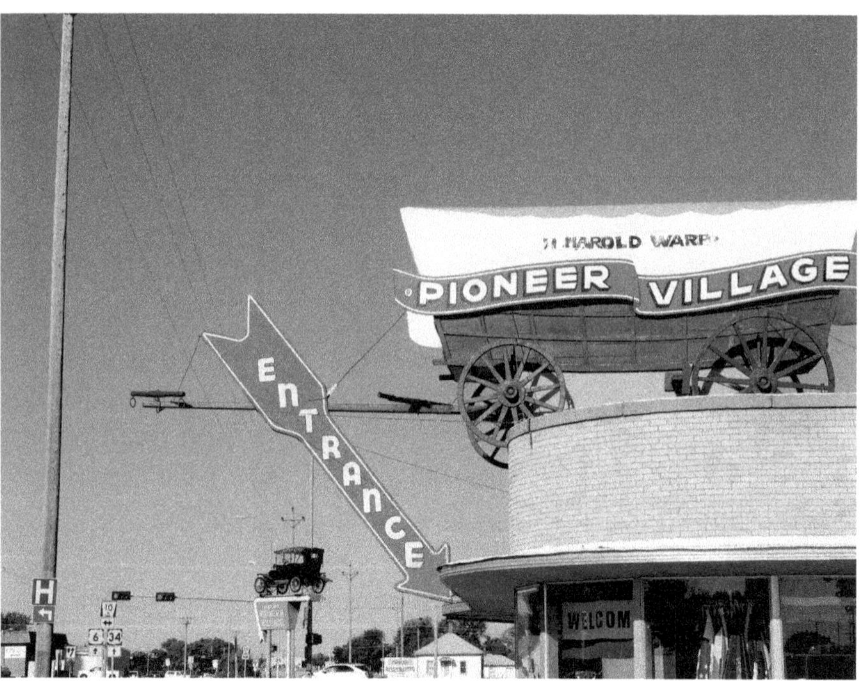

Pioneer Village in Minden displays America's progress in recent centuries.

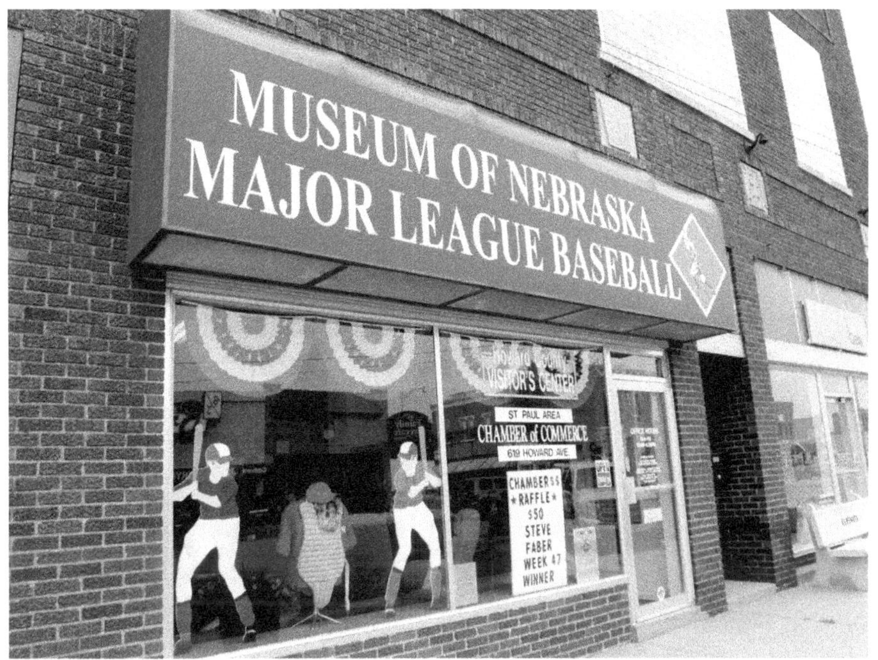

Over 140 professional baseball players with Nebraska ties are featured at the Museum of Nebraska Major League Baseball.

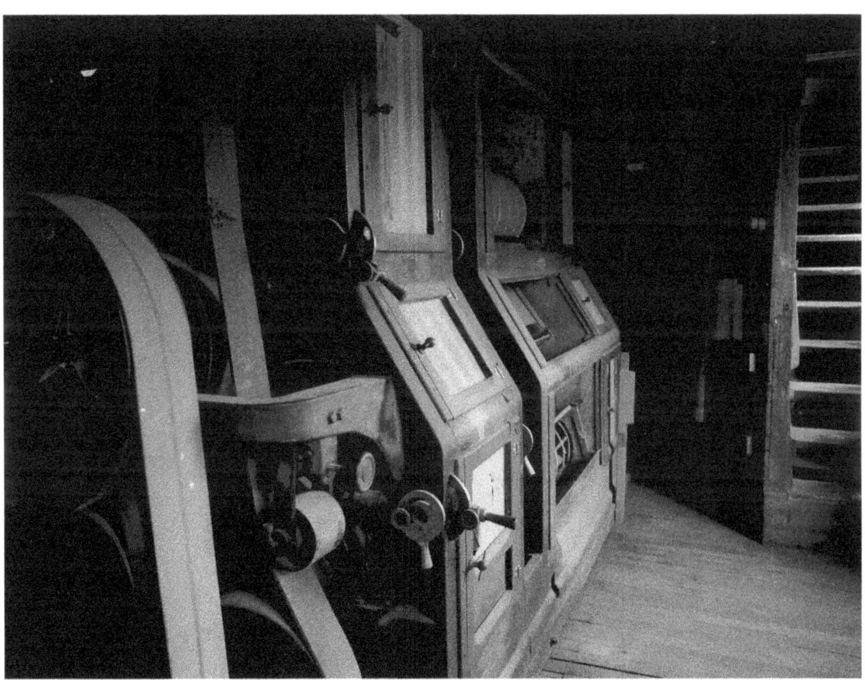

Area residents give tours of the historic mill in Champion.

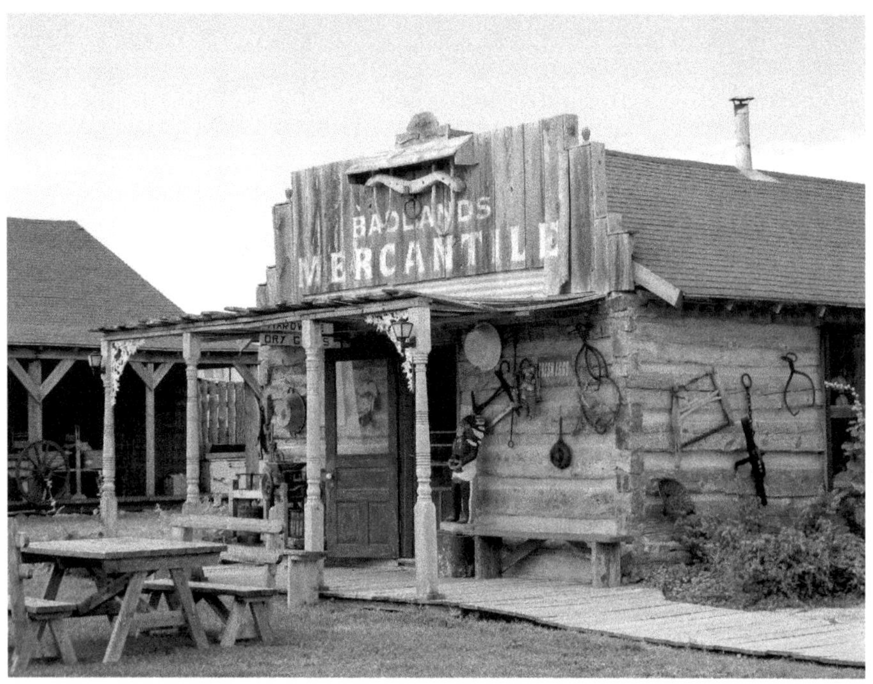

This Badlands Mercantile is one of several buildings relocated to the High Plains Homestead near Crawford.

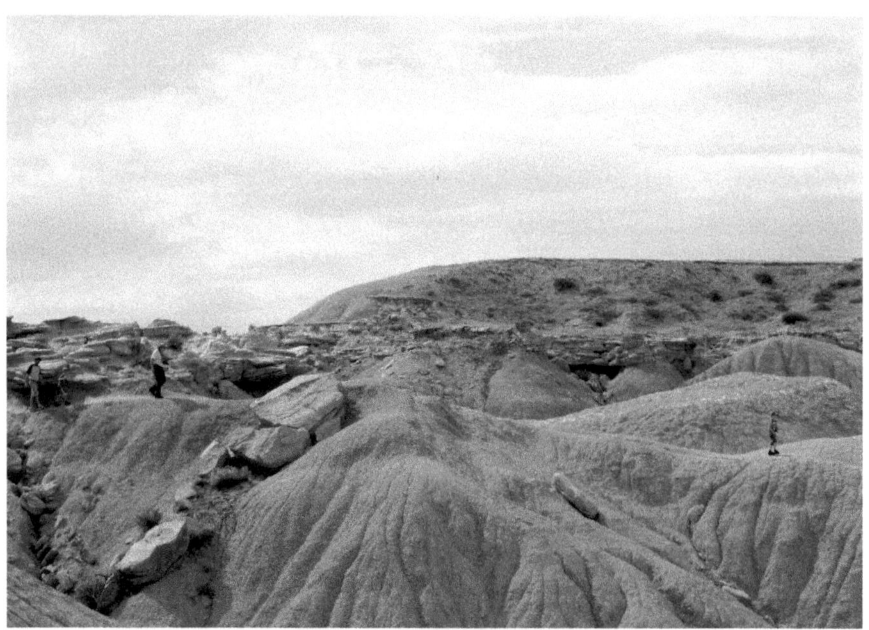

Hikers at Toadstool Geological Park are treated to unique land formations rarely found anywhere else.

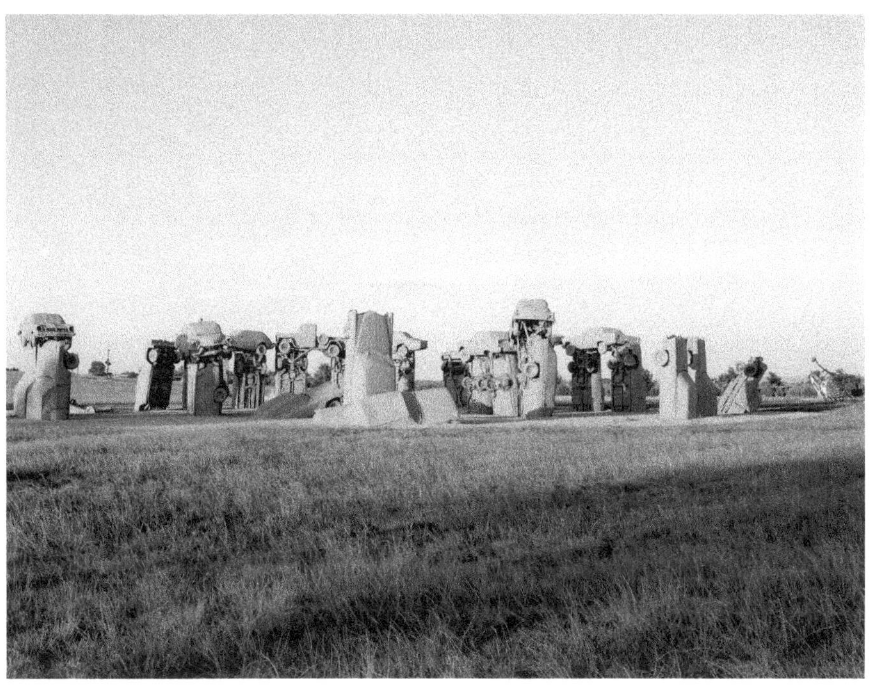

Constructed in 1987, Carhenge was modeled after England's ancient Stonehenge.

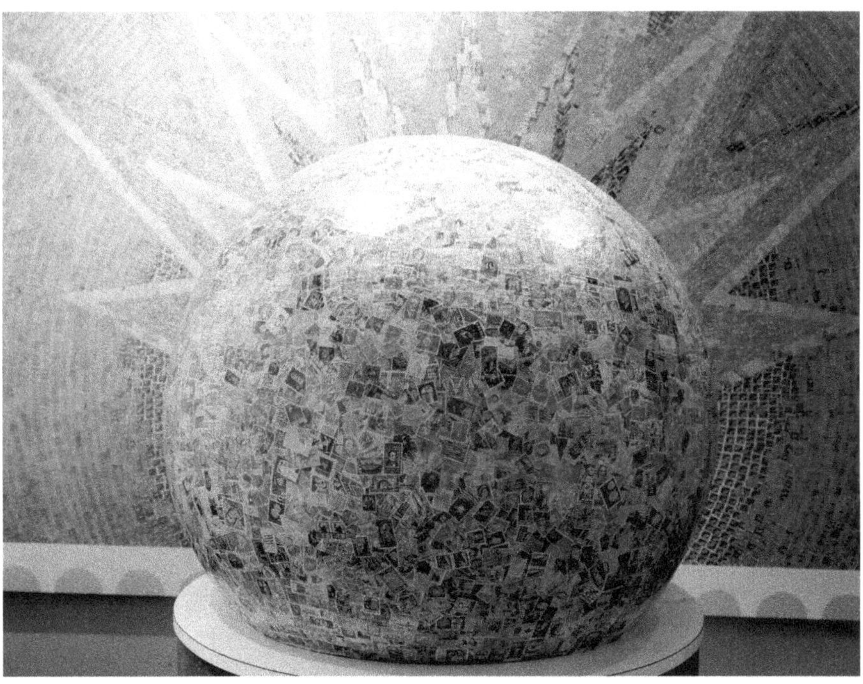

Formed from 4,655,000 stamps, the world's largest stamp ball is at Boys Town.

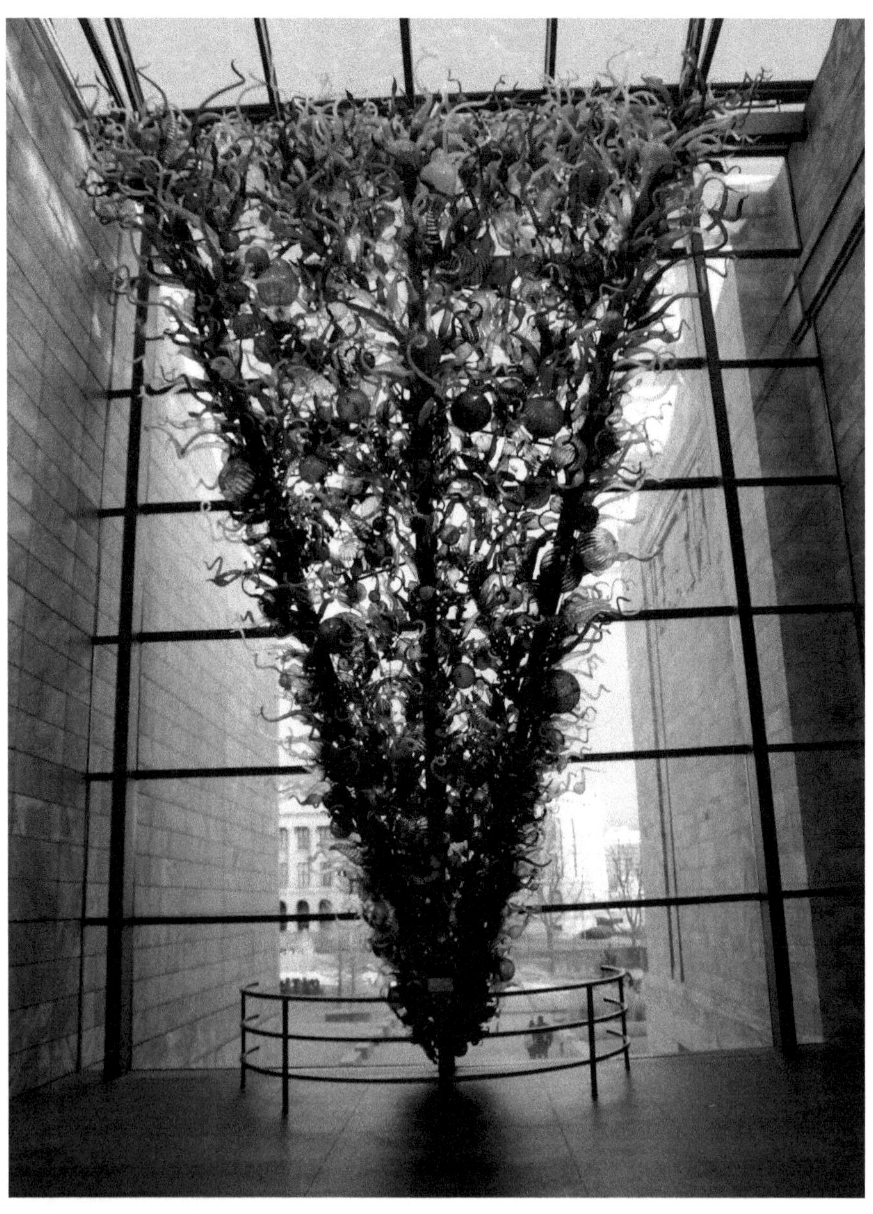

The *Chihuly Inside and Out* sculpture became a part of Omaha's Joslyn Art Gallery in 2000.

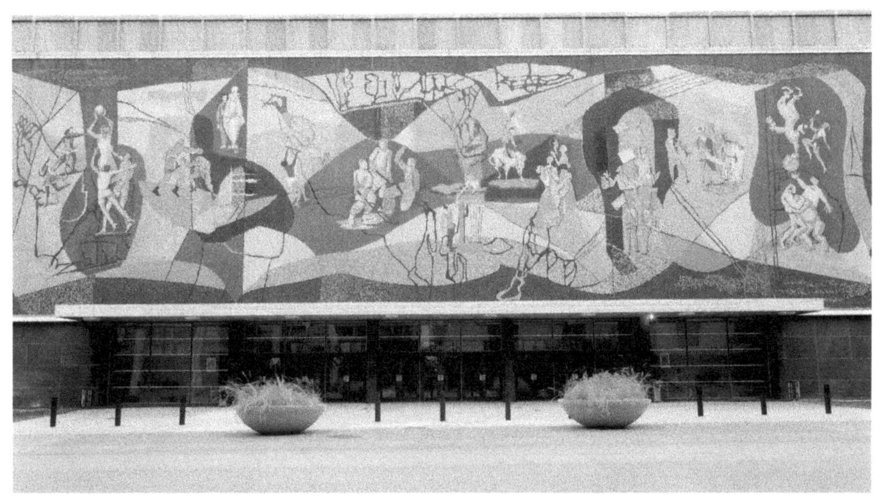

Lincoln's Pershing mural has almost 800,000 pieces of tile.

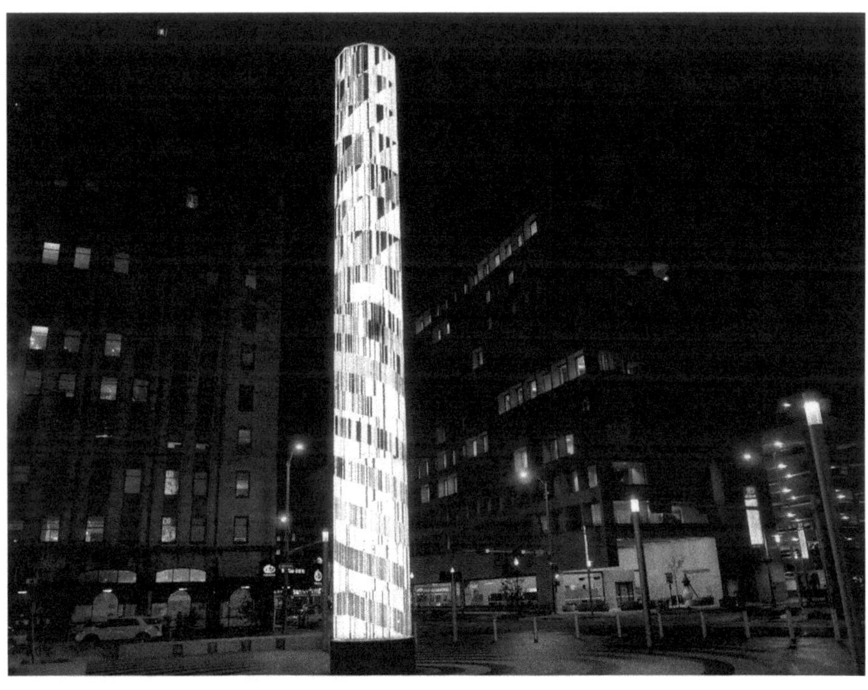

Ascent at Tower Square in downtown Lincoln was created by Omaha artist Jun Kaneko in 2014.

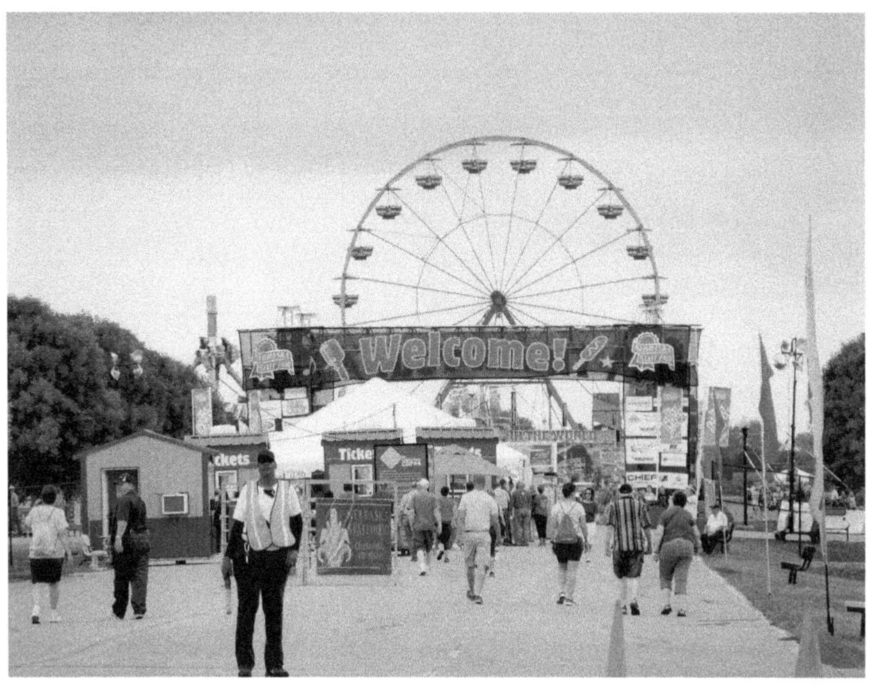

Formerly in Lincoln, the Nebraska State Fair moved to Grand Island in 2010.

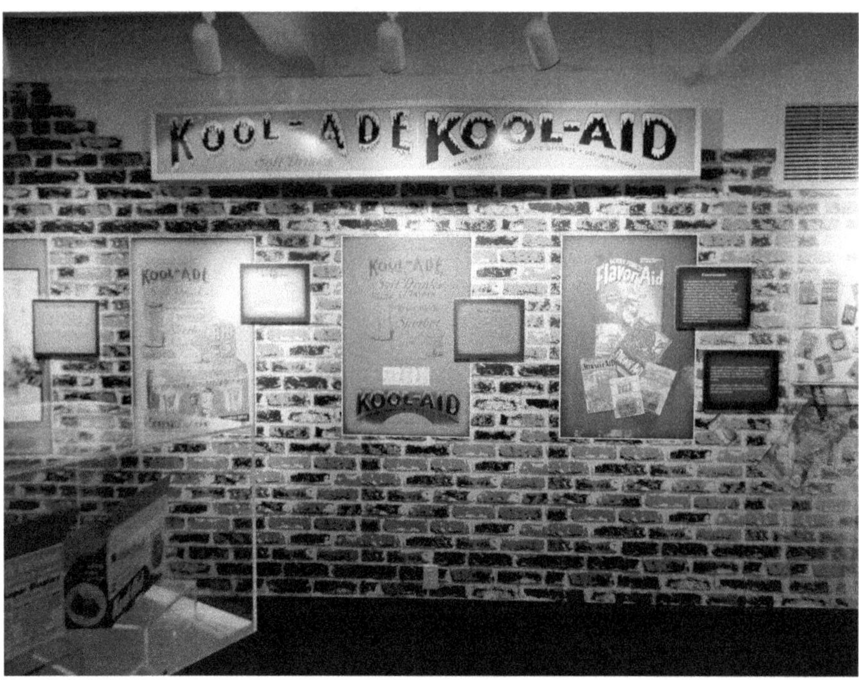

One Hastings Museum exhibit features Kool-Aid and its Hastings inventor, Edwin Perkins.

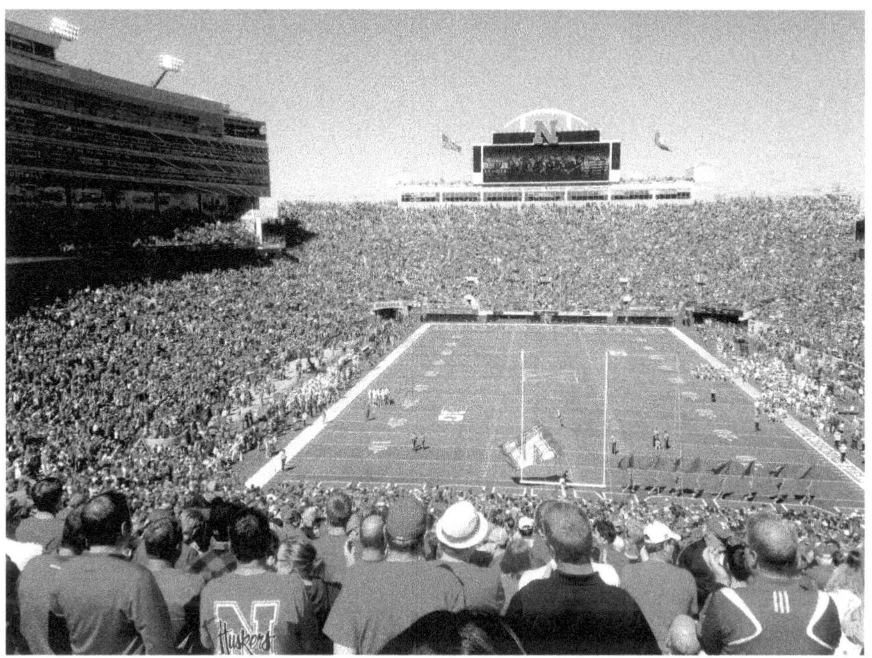

With over eighty-five thousand Nebraska Husker fans attending each home football game, Memorial Stadium temporarily becomes the state's third-largest city.

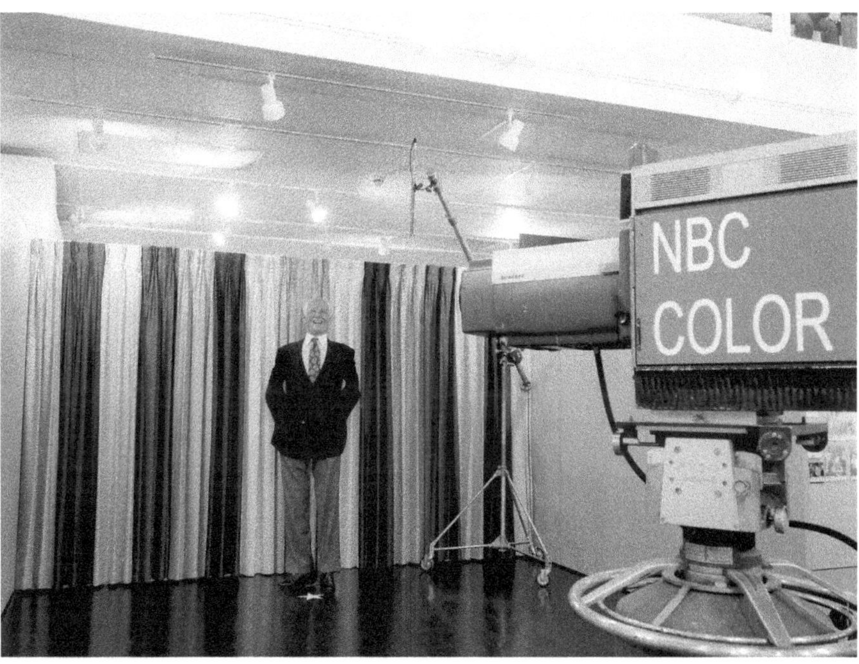

Norfolk's Elkhorn Valley museum presents Johnny Carson, hometown hero and one of late-night television's funniest comedians.

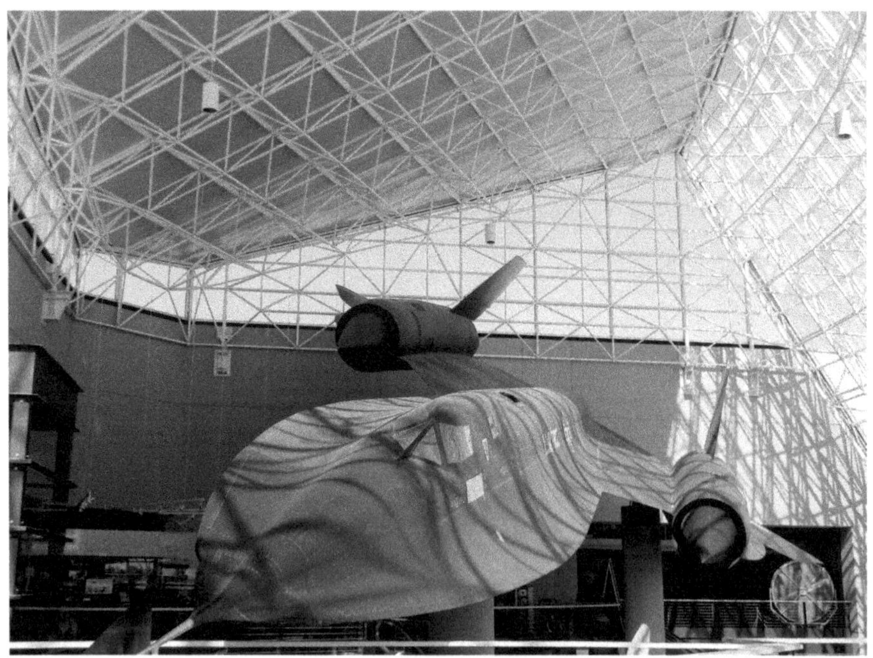

The SR-TIA "Blackbird" is still flying high at the Strategic Air Command and Aerospace.

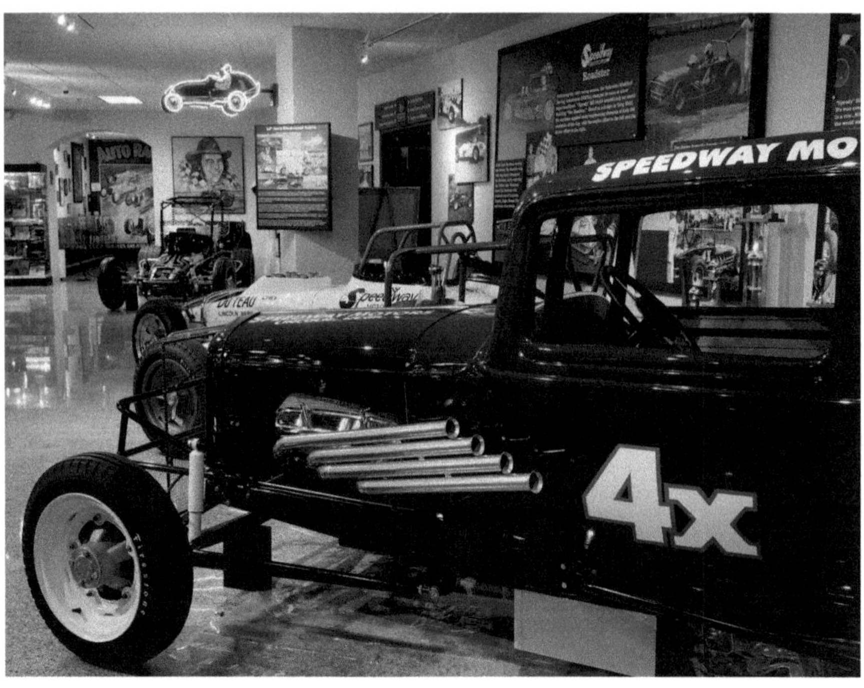

The Speedway Motors Museum of American Speed exhibits include automobiles raced by collector "Speedy" Bill Smith's own drivers.

were donated to the site. The property's transformation is staggering. In 2007, the educational programs began.

This location near Hastings gives city kids opportunities to experience agriculture firsthand. Field trips and family programs happen often. Outdoor camps allow kids to become farmhands for the day. Springfest and Harvestfest are annual events. At the Flatwater Music Festival, patrons enjoy the farm in a whole new way. Connecting visitors to the state's agricultural roots is the goal.

Prairie Loft also teaches conservation, as protecting natural resources requires education. What better way is there to learn than experiencing the results firsthand? In the future, the location hopes to expand. By providing onsite experiences and online resources, Prairie Loft is teaching the next generations to value the land.

WILLA CATHER IN RED CLOUD AND BEYOND

The country and I had it out together. By the end of the first autumn, that shaggy grass country had gripped me with a passion I have never been able to shake. It has been the happiness and the curse of my life.
—Willa Cather

When they moved from Virginia, Willa Cather and her family arrived to a new, stark land. Nebraska had only been a state for sixteen years and was far from settled. Nine-year-old Willa first caught glimpses of this wild prairie through the windows of a train. Her new home was near Red Cloud. Little did she know that this move would inspire her and others for years to come.

Besides their personal belongings, the only item to make the trip with them was her mother's china. Cather's father farmed for a season, but the family moved to town for better schooling and opportunities. Throughout all her new life experiences, Cather would connect with the people, especially the immigrants and the prairie pioneers. The tales that she heard would help her write stories of her own.

After her high school graduation, Cather left to attend the university in Lincoln. Her goal was to be a doctor. But her college freshman English teacher saw a different potential path for Cather and even submitted one of Cather's essays to a newspaper. Upon its publication, Cather changed her career aspirations. Soon she was a writer, then editor of the school newspaper and the yearbook. Her articles were published in the *Lincoln Courier*. Reviews for the *Nebraska State Journal* kept her busy. Cather immersed herself in the literary world.

After graduation, she returned to Red Cloud for a year. Once the East Coast publishing world called out to her, she left town and never lived there again. Journalism came first. Then Cather began to write poetry and fiction. Her second novel, *O Pioneers!*, put both Cather and Red Cloud on the map.

Although Cather's address changed, she never left her roots. Even though the small towns in her books were given different names, essentially each one was Red Cloud. Her experiences on the prairie also influenced many of her stories. Six of her novels would be set in Nebraska. Featuring immigrants on the plains, *My Ántonia* might be Cather's most well-known book. Cather's connection to her childhood experiences helped to capture a time that might have been forgotten.

Visiting Red Cloud Today

Within a decade of Cather's death in 1947, the town of Red Cloud made a move to protect its part in Cather's legacy. The Willa Cather Pioneer Memorial, now known as the Willa Cather Foundation, formed to preserve both her personal and literary legacy. Over the past several decades, that purpose has been refined and expanded.

Available tours demonstrate Cather's influence in Red Cloud. Visitors can choose to visit three or seven historical town buildings on designated

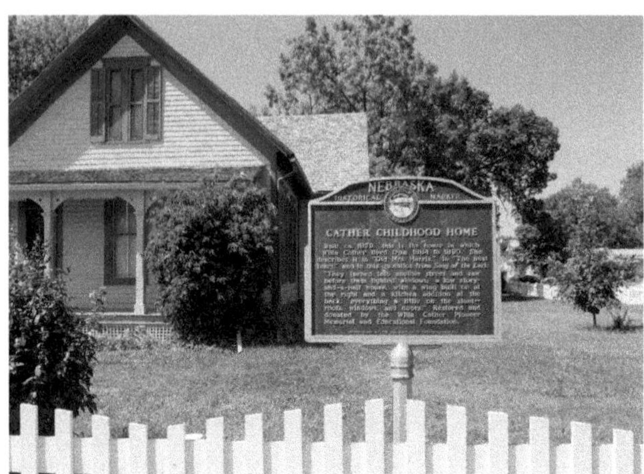

Author Willa Cather's childhood home in Red Cloud is one of many preserving her legacy.

tours. Willa Cather's childhood home, a National Historic Landmark, is on both itineraries. "Cather in the Country" tours encompass sixty miles and highlight twenty-one points of interest. To take this driving tour, please set up an appointment. Outside of town, the Willa Cather Memorial Prairie features native grasses and nature opportunities.

Recently, the Willa Cather Foundation opened the National Willa Cather Center. Along with an arts and cultural center, a new museum and archive area are open. Literary events take place often. The gift shop sells Cather's books and other memorabilia. Staff and volunteers are dedicated to continuing Cather's legacy.

Above the foundation offices, the Red Cloud Opera House is still serving the community. Varied performances include plays, concerts, humanities presentations, gallery exhibits and more. Professionals and community members provide entertainment.

FURNAS-GOSPER COUNTIES

In the small town of Arapahoe, local history is valued. First, the Furnas-Gosper Museum presents past events from both counties. Nearby, the Arapahoe Pharmacy fosters a nostalgic history all its own. At first glance, this location seems to be an ordinary drugstore. But the marble counter lining most of the east wall tells another tale. For decades, patrons have been quenching their thirst at the store's soda fountain. Take a spin on the red vinyl stools and try out a classic drink for yourself. Getting to have a green river phosphate again brought me back to my childhood. Always wondered what a "black and white" tastes like? This is the place to become enlightened.

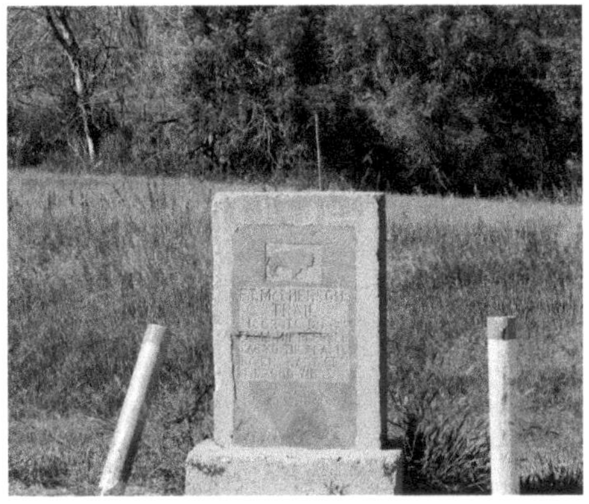

During an 1869 military campaign, this trail connected Platte Valley's Fort McPherson to the Republican River Valley.

NEBRASKA PRAIRIE MUSEUM IN HOLDREGE

Waving tall grasses sway gently as far as the eye can see. Although parts of Nebraska are hilly, this section of land is flat. It is wide-open prairie waiting to be plowed. The settlers made this land come to life. Even today, the fields surrounding the Nebraska Prairie Museum complex are harvested. Outside of Holdrege, stories are presented about the community.

Formerly the Phelps County Museum, this location's displays go far beyond one county. The eclectic collections include Native American artifacts, china sets, antique farm implements, classic automobiles and vintage toys. The Lindgren library allows researchers to discover their part in area history.

Tour an American small town square. Around the museum are many replicated shops. See the former Holdrege post office. Browse the items for sale in the general store. Both the fire and police departments of former days are represented. Walking through these rooms brings history to life.

Once in the country, the District 66 "Snowball" schoolhouse is now here. The former Sam Anderson farmhouse provides a glimpse into simpler times. Depending on timing, visitors may see an actual bride and groom. Weddings still take place at this old Lutheran church building.

One display pays tribute to an unexpected part of Nebraska history. Only miles from town, Camp Atlanta once housed prisoners of war. During World War II, these foreign men were forced to help with farming. Labor was lacking due to local men fighting across the seas. Being a prisoner in Nebraska was a blessing. Even then, hardworking Nebraskans treated strangers well.

Guarding museum grounds is a Camp Atlanta replica watchtower. Inside is the POW Interpretative Center. Photographs of the prisoners of war line the walls. Items used during their encampment show what life was like. Even letters offer a glimpse into the story. War posters claiming victory remind visitors of this patriotic time.

The Thomas F. Naegel Art Gallery presents Nebraska's part in World War II in a different light. Naegel immigrated to this country from Germany at the age of sixteen. After being drafted, he went to Camp Atlanta as an interpreter. Following the war, he captured his memories in a series of artworks. Titled *The Eye of the Storm*, his pieces provide insight into the war experience in Nebraska. Between the European and Pacific fronts, Nebraska was paradise for these German men.

My maternal grandmother grew up in this area. She and her siblings made a quilt out of old family neckties. This covering is now a part of the

Nebraska Prairie Museum collection. In 2007, this necktie quilt was included in the "Going West: Quilts and Community" display. The Smithsonian's Renwick Gallery hosted the exhibit. In 2007, ninety-three Holen family members traveled together to Washington, D.C., to see the family quilt in its temporary home.

The Heartland Museum of Military Vehicles (HMMV) in Lexington

Ever wondered what sitting in a tank would be like? This central Nebraska location encourages exploration of all vehicles on display. Besides tanks, helicopters, halftracks and even ambulances are on display. Jeeps from every branch of service are lined up. From World War II to present day, about one hundred restored vehicles are ready for action. Most are still operational. Military engines are also housed here.

In addition to vehicles, displays include supplies necessary to a soldier's life. Exhibits include uniforms worn, weapons once carried, equipment, supplies needed for battle and even MREs. Encased in a glass display are hundreds of patches designating rank and file. Recently, the museum set up a MASH (mobile hospital) exhibit. The USS *Lexington* aircraft carrier is highlighted through photographs and memorabilia. Kids of all ages will enjoy seeing the corporal teddy bears set around the museum. This location is open year round. Donations help this museum continue to expand.

Cozad

When John J. Cozad traveled west on the Union Pacific Railroad, a plaque caught his eye. To him "The 100th Meridian" was a sign of another kind. This location where the humid East meets the arid West seemed to be a great place to start a new town. Returning to Ohio, he convinced friends to join him. Soon after that 1872 visit, Cozad was an official Nebraska town. Growth happened quickly. Beside the railroad tracks, Cozad's hotel was a big draw.

Grasshoppers almost derailed the town. In fact, many packed up and left. But Cozad was determined to keep his town alive.

He built more businesses and a school. When his funds ran out, he often looked to gambling to help him "earn" more money. His hot temper would cost him the town—or at least the right to live there. During an argument with a local, Cozad drew his gun. The shot proved fatal, as the man died two months later. Cozad fled Cozad, and his wife and sons followed with their money sewn into their clothes. From then on, the Cozads lived elsewhere.

The 100th Meridian Museum and More

This museum tells more of Cozad's story. The antique popcorn stand that once provided townspeople with snacks is outside. The extensive Memorial Wall honors area veterans. Photographs document lives from another time. The museum's prized stagecoach arrived from the West. In that Yellowstone touring coach, President William Howard Taft and family once traveled through that park. Now Cozad citizens ride inside. At the Atkinson Hay Days celebration and at North Platte Nebraska Days, the coach travels the parade routes.

Robert Henri Museum

Art cannot be separated from life. It is the expression of the greatest need of which life is capable, and we value art not because of the skilled product, but because of its revelation of a life's experience.

—Robert Henri

Born right after the end of the Civil War, Robert Henry Cozad started life in the East. In 1873, his father founded Cozad, Nebraska, so the family moved west. Spending his childhood summers on the prairie gave Cozad a different perspective on people. This stint in rural America would influence his artwork in later days. Forced to leave Cozad due to his father's poor choices, the Cozads changed their names. At this point, Robert became Robert Henri. Pronounced "Hen-rye," little did Robert know that this would be the perfect name for an up-and-coming artist.

After the family ended up on the East Coast, Henri began painting. Attending the Pennsylvania Academy of Fine Arts in Philadelphia furthered his skills. For two years, he studied vigorously under experts. Soon Henri recognized that to extend his training, he needed to go to Europe. While studying abroad, his style moved toward impressionism. When he moved back to America, Cozad became an art teacher at several East Coast schools. He never forgot Paris and returned there often. Later, his fascination changed to Ireland; he spent spring and summer there.

As his art grew bolder, so did his philosophy. He embraced an art that was real, and this set him apart. In 1908, he organized *The Eight*, an exhibit at Macbeth Gallery in New York that included seven other artists. Later, this exhibition was considered to be the start of the Ashcan School movement. This style of art was grittier and truer to life. Henri's revolution altered the art world, and he was honored for his progressiveness. The Arts Council of New York put his name on an important list in the spring of 1929. In their eyes, he was one of the top three living American artists of the time. Ironically, he would die that very summer from cancer.

Today, the Robert Henri Museum is housed in Henri's former childhood home. Over the years, the house changed hands often, but citizens concerned with preserving Cozad history bought the property. Transforming the home into a museum took a considerable amount of effort and wallpaper removal. After much research, volunteers collected Cozad family personal items; many of Henri's hand-composed letters are also on display. Being at this location gives visitors a glimpse into Henri's childhood, and thoroughly researched genealogy tells about the founding family's roots.

As for Henri's art, it is not in short supply either. The museum contains the largest collection of Henri artwork in the world. Six oil paintings and thirty-three sketches are a part of the permanent collection. The Robert Henri Gallery is housed in a secure climate-controlled building. Slides document collections containing two hundred of his works. This museum connects Henri's life and his art. Henri would be pleased by the result.

Travel the Robert Henri Historic Walkway to see more remnants from the past. The reconstructed Willow Island Pony Express Station now sits at the Veteran's Memorial Park. The Little Church by the Park moved nearby as well. Now that building hosts art shows and small gatherings. Also at the park is the pioneer school formerly known as Adle School.

GOTHENBURG DELIVERS

Once southwest of Gothenburg, the Sam Machette station was a busy location. Built in 1854, the site was a trading post and ranch house along the Oregon Trail. From 1860 to 1861, the small plank cabin became a Pony Express station. After being moved to Gothenburg's Ehmen Park in 1931, the building was saved from deterioration. Twenty-three years later, the station opened again as the Pony Express Museum. Complete with a cookstove and an antique desk filled with lists of actual riders, this cabin teaches about Pony Express history. Behind glass are actual artifacts. Framed photographs allude to another time.

Not every place displays life-sized barbed-wire sculptures. At the Sod House Museum near the I-80 exit, these creations add interest. A replica sod house is on site. In the reproduction barn is memorabilia reflecting the challenges faced by pioneers. Farther into town the Gothenburg Historical Museum presents more about local history. All three Gothenburg museums are free, but donations are appreciated.

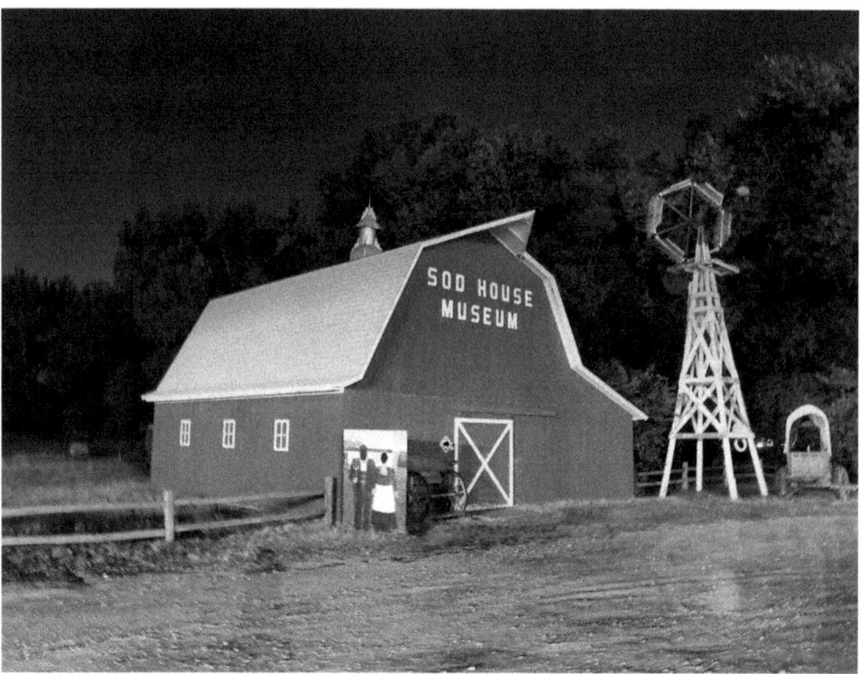

The Sod House Museum in Gothenburg honors early settlers.

6
PRAIRIE LAKES

Although rain is not plentiful in this part of Nebraska, reservoirs are. Lakes—including the state's largest, Lake McConaughy—were created to help with water management. This part of Nebraska is known for boating and fishing. Recreational opportunities abound here, as does a history that includes skirmishes as well as settlers determined to stay.

Fort McPherson National Cemetery Near Maxwell

Cottonwood Canyon needed a site that would guard those on the Overland Trail and those constructing the railroad. Fort McKean, later named Fort McPherson, provided that. From 1863 to 1880, this fort provided protection. In 1873, the government determined that this central location was ideal for a national cemetery. Forty acres were set aside, and soldiers killed at remote posts would be buried here. When the fort closed, the cemetery stayed.

Today, almost four thousand graves are at this site. Some of the earliest remains are in a mass grave. The Sioux killed twenty-eight soldiers at Fort Laramie in 1854. Known as the Grattan Massacre, this event started the conflicts between the Native Americans and white men in the region. Sixty-three buffalo soldiers were also moved to this location. Not all soldiers buried here were killed deliberately. Six soldiers perished in an 1873 flash flood that filled their Republican Valley campsite. From before the Civil War to beyond, soldiers have found their final resting place here. Even today, former military and their families can be buried at Fort McPherson National Cemetery.

North Platte

In 1866, the Union Pacific Railroad started setting rails near the Platte River. To entice the tracks to come to their area, two men built a general store. Setting it north of the Platte gave the town its start and its name. Construction crews overwintered in the new town, but this made for a rough start. With saloons and plenty of gambling, the first residents needed a tolerance for noise and for danger. North Platte had the distinction of being known as the first "Hell on Wheels" town.

Once the railroad tracks went farther west, North Platte changed its reputation. The completed roundhouse provided respectable railroad jobs. Once a school and a jailhouse were built, North Platte became more of a settlement. The cattle trail also brought settlers to town. Both the railroad and cowboys continue to transform North Platte into a strong town today.

Every third week in June, North Platte's population doubles during NEBRASKAland Days. Featured is the Buffalo Bill Rodeo. Classic car displays and woodcarving demonstrations take place. Kids can try mutton busting, sandcastle building or simply enjoy playing at the fun festival. During the weekend, concerts with country music headliners take place.

The Railyard

For over a century, passengers traveled the rails through North Platte. Union Pacific's chief engineer, Grenville Dodge, was instrumental in establishing the railroad junction here. Between the flat topography and proximity to water, North Platte became a significant railroad town.

Still today, Bailey Yard is the largest classification rail yard in the world. With fourteen thousand rail cars passing through daily, this location encompasses almost three thousand acres. To make this possible, the rail yard never closes. Repairs, servicing and fueling also happen at this rail yard.

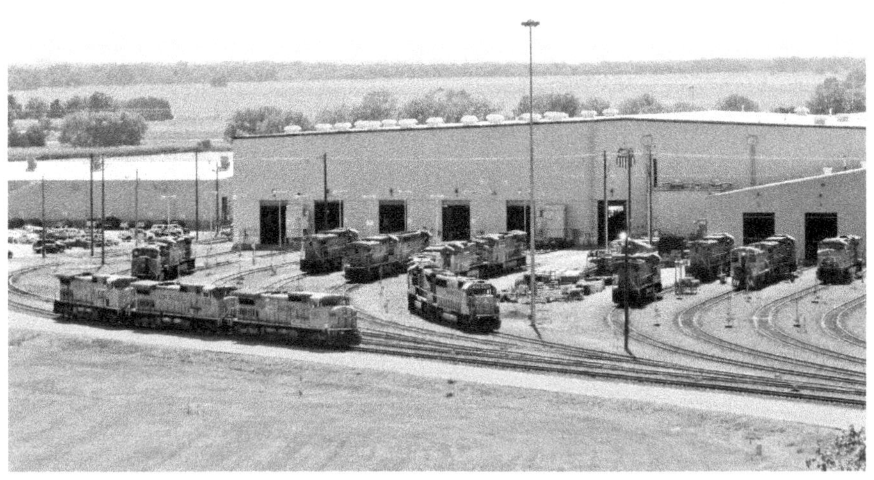

Bailey Yard North Platte is the world's largest rail yard. *Photo by Tim Trudell.*

While the Union Pacific and Central Pacific Railroads met in Utah, North Platte has a railroad distinction of its own. The East meets the West on the Union Pacific line at this location. Promontory Point has the golden spike, and North Platte has the Golden Spike Tower.

The Golden Spike Tower and Visitor Center

In the 1990s, some North Platte community boosters decided Bailey Yard needed to be more accessible to visitors. Railroad enthusiasts from around the world wanted to make the pilgrimage to see this classification yard. To connect the people to the tracks again, an eight-story observation tower was completed in 2006. Even though the center is next to the railroad, the town of North Platte is responsible for the site.

In the lobby, a model train chugs above visitors as a reminder of the relevance of this location. The hall of fame brings the early railroaders to life; train enthusiasts can find souvenirs.

Up in the tower, the railroad comes to life for visitors. On the seventh floor, visitors can wander among open observation decks. Sliding rail cars and the roar of locomotives convey the high activity level found here. Besides a full view of the yard, the fully enclosed eighth floor offers a completely different experience. Scattered exhibits convey railroad facts and history in an interactive way. Often, retired railroad workers volunteer as tour guides. Learning from those who worked on site is the best way to find out more about the functionality of this railroad location.

Outside, twenty-three state flags fly high, representing the states through which the Union Pacific passes. The Brick Pavilion Wall commemorates many railroad and community members. On site, a vintage dining car is being restored. Touring this will provide visitors with a taste of riding the rails in the style.

Every third weekend in September, North Platte hosts a Rail Days event. This weekend is the only time that guests can go out on the rail yard itself. Beforehand, visitors must buy a designated ticket. In town, Cody Park provides tours of outdoor locomotives, rail cars and a caboose. On site is a restored train depot.

Buffalo Bill Ranch State Historical Park

On July 4, 1882, Buffalo Bill Cody planned quite the performance. The Old Glory Blowout in North Platte featuring western showmen and Native Americans was a big success, signaling the beginning of his Wild West Show. For several decades, Cody took his show on the road. Proximity to the railroad made Cody's productions possible. In 1886, Cody built a home base on the edge of North Platte. At one time, his ranch included four thousand acres. His home, which he named Scout's Rest, became a retreat for his family until they moved to Wyoming in 1913.

In 1965, the State of Nebraska acquired and restored this property. Scout's Rest is a part of the 16-acre Buffalo Bill Ranch Historical Park. During warmer months, several buildings, complete with Cody's personal effects, are open. A small admission fee is charged to tour the home. The adjacent Buffalo Bill State Recreation Area encompasses 250 acres. To visit either area, a Nebraska state park permit is necessary.

THE NORTH PLATTE CANTEEN

During World War II, the haunting sounds of a train whistle signified soldiers going off to war. On December 17, 1941, local residents heard their boys were passing through on their way to training camp. Loaded down with Christmas packages, family and friends met Company D. Confusion resulted when the train held Kansas guardsmen. Rather than returning home, locals passed out the presents anyway. The look of joy and disbelief on the strangers' faces gave Rae Wilson an idea. She spearheaded an effort to welcome more troop trains to town. Supplies were gathered, and volunteers signed up to help.

On Christmas Day 1941, the North Platte Canteen was officially set in motion. Women met the train with baskets of goodies. Due to restrictions, at first the treats were passed through train windows to the soldiers. As World War II went forward, the number of trains increased. Eventually, the depot lunchroom became canteen headquarters. During the ten-minute stops, soldiers would disembark for a free hot meal. With over twenty daily trains, thousands of meals were served during the course of the war.

This required sacrifices for the completely volunteer effort. Rationing of sugar was in place, yet about twenty cakes per day were still served to any birthday boy. Gas was also limited, but volunteers came from over one hundred area towns. Some traveled up to two hundred miles. Over the five-year operation, fifty-five thousand people served the six million soldiers who came to town. Not a single train was missed.

At the Lincoln County Historical Society Museum, one room showcases this amazing volunteer effort. Under a glass display, a table is set with dishes and food, and photographs chronicle the experience. Although North Platte never built munitions, it did serve up morale.

FORT CODY TRADING POST

Those traveling in the middle of Nebraska on Interstate 80 cannot help but notice the giant fort reproduction at the Highway 83 exit. For over sixty years, Fort Cody has been Nebraska's largest western gift shop. Complete with nostalgic and unique items not found anywhere else, be prepared to be amused.

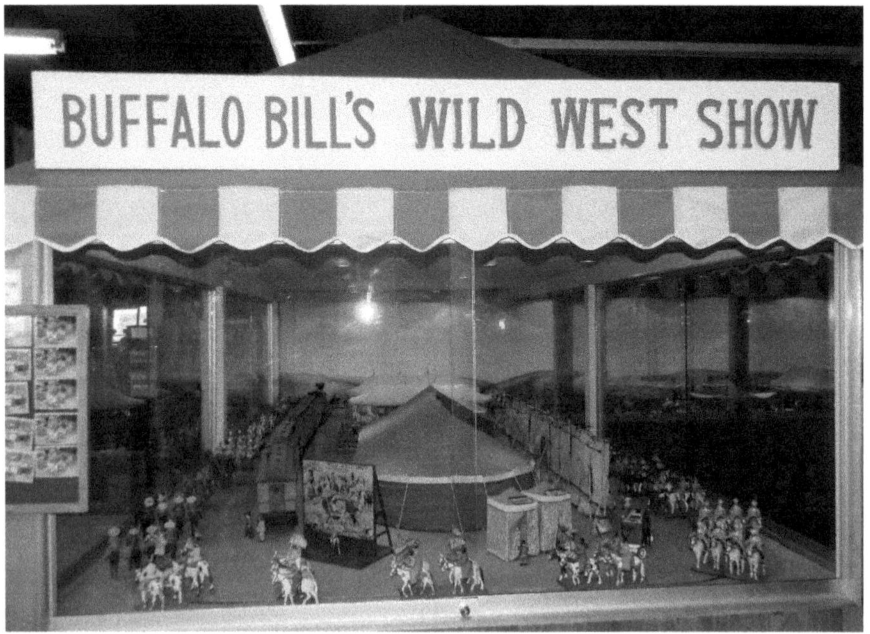

Carving this twenty-thousand-piece Buffalo Bill Wild West Show replica took Ernie and Virginia Palmquist twelve years.

More than a gift shop, this destination could almost be considered a museum. The Buffalo Bill's Wild West Show in Miniature is prominently on display. Twenty thousand hand-carved and painted pieces were created by Ernie and Virginia Palmquist. This large replica is observable behind glass. The figures are motorized and perform the show. Behind the building, travelers can explore the outdoor stockade. Kids of all ages enjoy "going to jail." A Native American "muffler men" giant statue and a two-headed stuffed calf provide more photo opportunities.

North Platte Fish Hatchery

Over twenty-one million fish are produced every year at this central Nebraska hatchery. Utilizing the Nebraska Public Power District irrigation system, water is recycled between forty-three ponds and the canal. Walleye, white bass and two catfish species are the typical species. Showing the collection of eggs gathered from regional water sites is a part of the public tours.

HERSHEY

Stones and Bones Gallery and Emporium

When your collected artifacts outgrow your home, why not start a museum? This became the path for a central Nebraska family. Their displays house everything from arrowheads to skulls. Artfully displayed, this location does bring western heritage to life. On the Stones and Bones website, photographs document finds and the scenery of this part of Nebraska. Admission is free, but calling in advance is recommended. As it states on the website, "Our hours are not chipped in stone."

McCOOK

Senator George Norris Historic Home

I loved the people I lived with and whom I had represented, and I had no idea of ever deserting them or leaving them.
—Senator George Norris in a letter to James E. Lawrence of the Lincoln Star

From 1902 to 1942, George W. Norris served Nebraska in Congress. Although he grew up in Ohio, after completing law school, he relocated to Nebraska at the age of twenty-four. He moved around the state until he finally settled in McCook.

During his time in Congress, Norris became known as the "Father of the TVA." The Tennessee Valley Authority's first dam project was named after him. Norris helped to form the Rural Electric Administration. He was also involved in fighting for agricultural concerns. Not only did Norris want to improve the lives of his fellow Nebraskans, but he also wanted to better the lives of all Americans.

Locally, Norris became the "Father of the Unicameral." In 1939, he convinced Nebraska voters to create a one-house body of government. By switching from a two-house system, Norris hoped to avoid partisanship. Even today, Nebraska state representatives are not elected under any particular political party.

Senator Norris and his family lived in the same McCook home for several decades. Over time, they updated rooms. Yet as visitors take a tour, they will

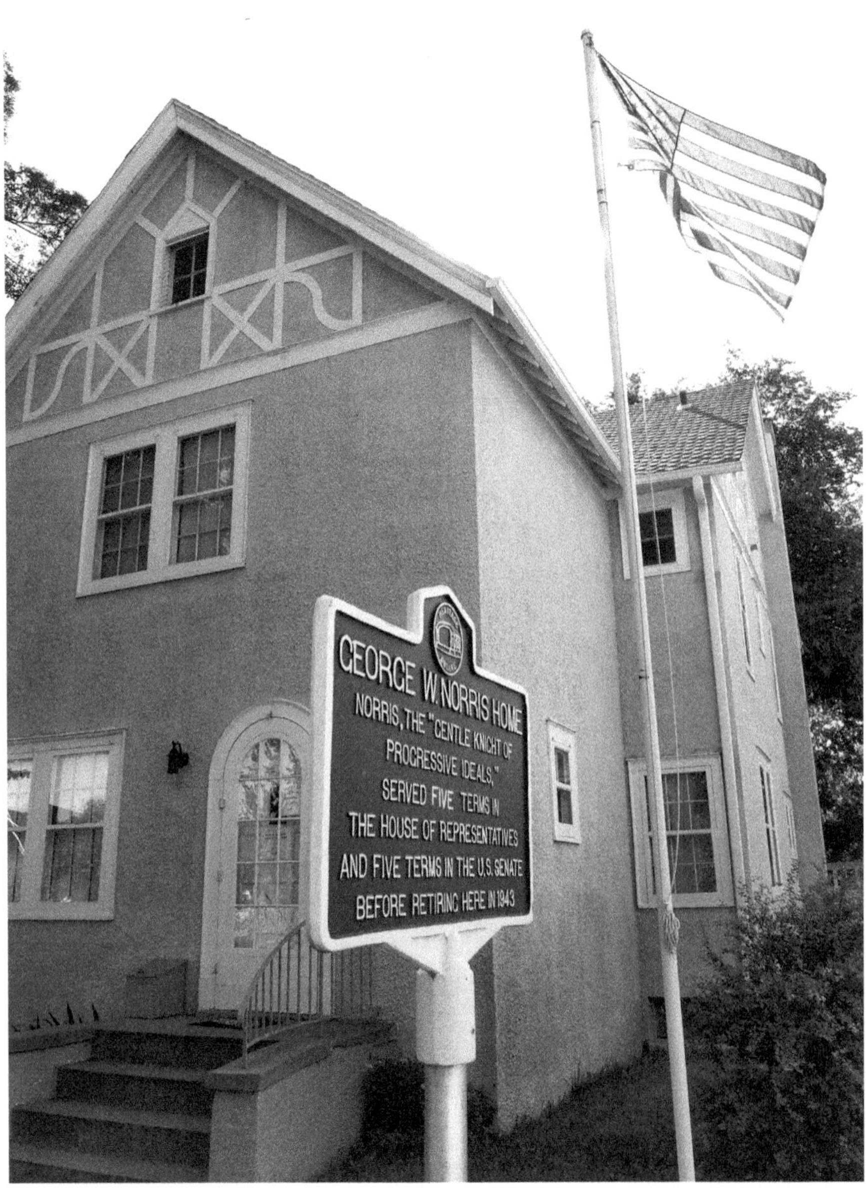

Senator George Norris's McCook home, his refuge during forty years in Congress, is open for tours.

feel as if they are walking back in time. When Mrs. George Norris donated their house to the state, she included the furnishings as well.

The interior woodwork still gleams. Laid out on the desk are the senator's spectacles and writing utensils as he might have left them. The study area seems to be waiting for Norris to appear. Even the household appliances remain the same. What might be the biggest treasure is tucked in the garage. Parked inside is a 1937 black Buick with a straight-8 engine and suicide doors. With the Norris family apparently in residence, visitors can get a true glimpse into their lives.

Palisade

Palisade may be a smaller Nebraska town, but its commitment to honoring servicemen and women is certainly mighty. On Main Street, a veterans' memorial honors all area veterans. Highlighted are those who served our country from the Civil War on. So far, over seven hundred names have been engraved on the five large granite stones.

Nearby is the monument to the POW camp that was once also found in this area. At various times near the end of World War II, additional laborers were needed to bring in the corn crop. German POWs were sent from the nearby Indianola Camp and were expected to fulfill that need. Although the remnants of the camp are no longer visible, the community still remembers. These foreign men helped them survive several harvests during the war. A marker notes the location of the former POW camp.

Massacre Canyon Monument

During Nebraska's earlier days, Native Americans still reigned in this part of the country. In the summer of 1873, three Pawnee tribal chiefs were leading their people on a buffalo hunt. Three hundred warriors and four hundred people strong, they were still warned to be wary of the nearby Sioux. On August 5, the Pawnee headed north between the Republican and Frenchman Rivers.

Sky Chief was the first Pawnee victim. As he was skinning a buffalo, the chief must not have anticipated the kill shot. The Pawnee began to scatter.

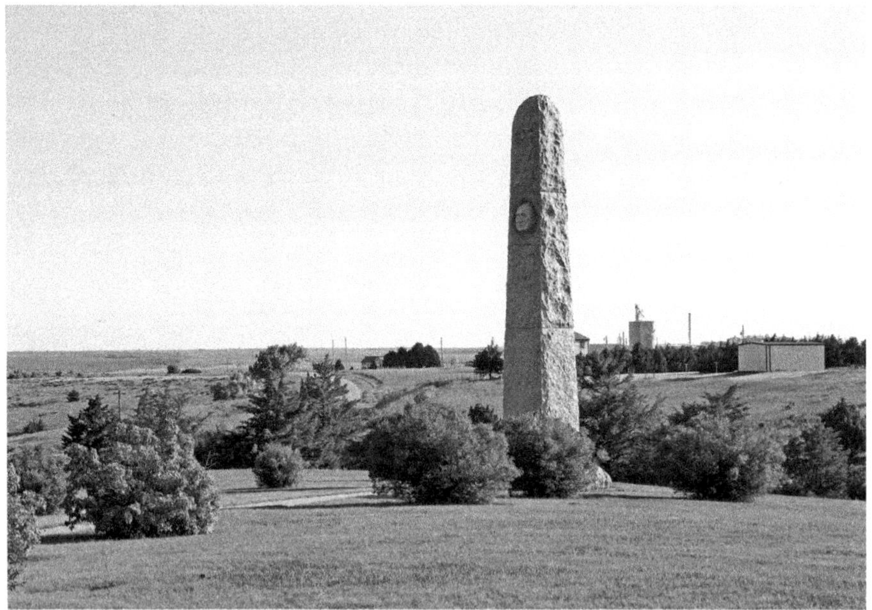

The Massacre Canyon monument marks the site of one of the last battles between the Pawnee and Sioux Indians.

Over the crest of the hill, a massive number of Sioux appeared. Clearly outnumbered four to one, a Pawnee warrior waved the white flag. His horse was shot from under him. The Sioux were on the warpath.

The Pawnee dropped everything and began to retreat. The women and children ran to a nearby canyon to hide. But the Sioux warriors followed, killing all in their paths. After the battle, the surviving Pawnee returned to their Loup River reservation. They never visited their hunting grounds again.

Today, a monument stands near the site of this last major battle. Due to excavating an adjacent Woodland Village from long ago, the memorial is not at the actual location. Instead, visitors overlook the place where the battle happened.

The thirty-five-foot-tall pink granite marker is near the town of Trenton. Carved near the top is a Sioux warrior, the victors in that battle. On the opposite side at a lower level, a carved Pawnee chief's face looks out. The 1873 August battle was the last and may have been the worst fight between the tribes. Ultimately, both tribes lost. This was the last of the Indian Wars. Soon after, Native Americans were forced to stay on reservations. The cattlemen would take over and thus win the land wars.

DUNDY COUNTY

Haigler residents are persistent about keeping town history alive. Three local sisters were so determined to help their community thrive that they were willing to spend the night in jail. As a part of a fundraiser, the sisters stayed in the cell overnight and requested bail money donations. That 1910 jail is now one of three town museums. At this Cornerstone Museum, displays highlight the contributions of farmers and ranchers.

In town, two former school buildings are educating in a new way. Once sitting quietly in a cornfield, the District 67 South small schoolhouse educated this section of farm community children. Thanks to the generosity of the farm family and area movers, the building was moved to Haigler for a minimal cost. Visitors can now see early Nebraska education displays at the one-room country schoolhouse. In the former historic Haigler elementary school is the newly established Cornerstone Center for Community Service. This location encourages gatherings.

Throughout the year, Haigler almost triples the population by hosting festivals. The Dundy Roo spring festival celebrates area art. During the summer, the Bluegrass Festival brings musical stylings to the park. At the fall Tumbleweed Festival, the town is decorated with figures created out of the dried plant. In the past, events have included community sales and even a chili cook-off. Rounding out the year is the Winter Holiday Festival. Ride along with Santa on the Reindeer Bus to see the Haigler Christmas lights. Community pride epitomizes Haigler.

Outside of town, more historic treasures await. Formerly known as the Goldenrod Highway, this section of Highway 34 was a bootleggers' route during the Prohibition era. The community hopes to restore the Highway name and the 1920s Conoco Station that would have been a popular spot then. Nearby is the start of the Nebraska section of the Great Western Cattle Trail. Craters and small canyons created by the cattle make driving the route impossible. Adventurous hikers can make that trek.

At Rock Creek, springs bubble up from the ground. In 1924, the Rock Creek Fish Hatchery began to help the Nebraska fish population. These abundant waters allow for production of both cold- and warm-water species. Nearly half of Nebraska's stocked trout are grown at this location. Visitors are welcome to tour during business hours.

Six miles west of Haigler is the Three Corners Tri-State Point. Travelers can stand in Nebraska, Kansas and Colorado all at the same time. This location is the start of the notable Arikree Breaks that continue down into Kansas. Heading back up toward central Nebraska, the Enders Reservoir makes for a beautiful rest stop.

Champion Historical Mill

For seventy years, a two-story flour mill served the small town of Champion in many ways. Starting in 1888, the mill produced high-quality flour. Using steel rollers along with sifting and regrounding gave this mill an edge. The original mill burned within a few years of opening. In 1892, the owner rebuilt on a stone foundation. Adding even more sophisticated machinery assured success. Sold several times, the mill continued grinding for decades.

The adjacent millpond provided for the community in another way. Recreational activities are popular here. In the 1920s, the owners built a diving board and a tall tower. At the bathhouse, suits were even rented for a dime. Boat rentals allowed visitors to enjoy the pond. Today, visitors bring their own boats. Even more show up with their fishing poles in hand.

For a time, this location was operated as a state historical park. Now the locals take care to keep up this site. On summer weekends, travelers can take a tour. A small room explains the history, and the original mill work is still housed inside.

Ole's Steakhouse in Paxton

With mounted animal heads looking on, travelers can enjoy a good steak dinner. This small-town eatery has a unique history. Ole's Steakhouse opened one minute past midnight on August 9, 1933, the day after Prohibition ended. Wanting to display the fruits of his travels, through the years Ole's mounted animal collection grew. The heads of over two hundred animals from around the world are now in central Nebraska.

OGALLALA

The Cowboy Capital of Nebraska

Known as the "town too tough for Texans," Ogallala was a rough place in its early days. Cattle drovers tried to forbid their cowboys from visiting the town, but many gunslingers still found their way to the streets. Fights often ended in fatalities.

Boothill Cemetery became a grave site in 1867, when three Union Pacific railroaders met their unfortunate end during an Indian raid. For fifteen years, this location was the town's official burying spot. Rolled inside canvas, over one hundred bodies were dumped into shallow graves. Nighttime burials of dead outlaws happened frequently. Many still had their boots on. Poor families with limited options also laid their dead to rest under the cover of darkness. The lucky ones were remembered with wooden headstones.

In 1886, Ogallala residents decided an actual cemetery was in order, as citizens desired decent burials. Four years later, the relocation of Boot Hill Cemetery began. When identifiable, the names and cause of death were recorded by an undertaker. This transfer of graves was not popular with the

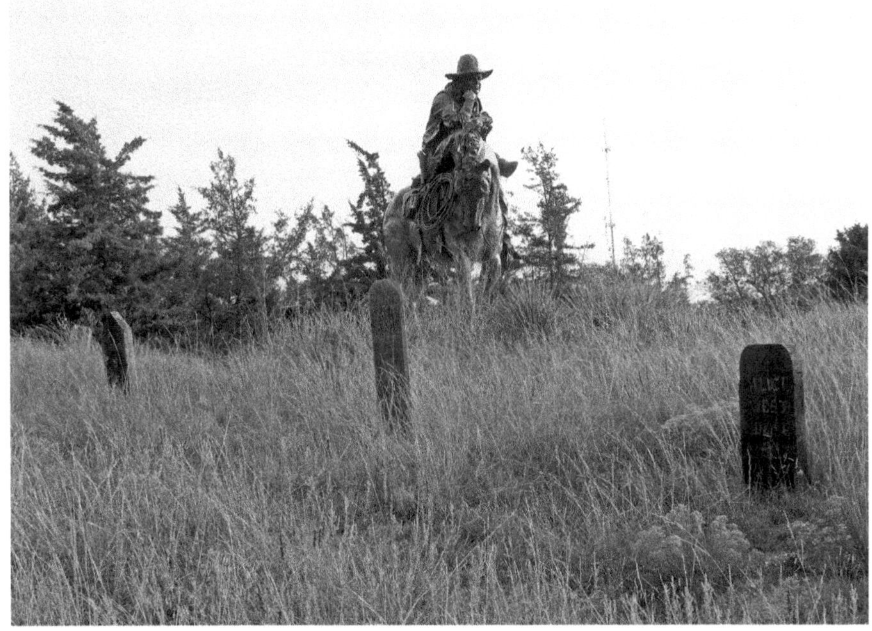

The Trail Boss at Ogallala's Boot Hill Cemetery represents Texas trail cattle drovers.

law-abiding crowd. Having their loved ones near outlaws, even after death, bothered many of them.

Although most remains were moved, visitors can still walk around the small Boot Hill Cemetery. Restored wooden headstones provide an explanation for the demise of some. Today, a gate surrounds the former burial site of a pioneer mother and child. A statue named *The Trail Boss* watches over these early settlers.

Mansion on the Hill

Around the time that the Boot Hill Cemetery occupants were moving out, new residents were moving in up the street. Finished in 1887, the Mansion on the Hill was considered the finest house in town. The local banker, Mr. McWilliams, and his wife were the original residents. With ten-foot ceilings, walnut shutters and two cherry wood fireplaces, the design was elaborate for the time. The carved door insets, panels and curved staircase are still lovely over a century later.

Today, visitors can tour this authentic Victorian home. An area schoolhouse also relocated to this property. Constructed in 1902, the District 7 school was first found five miles outside of Roscoe. This historic site is open from Memorial Day through Labor Day. Admission is free, but donations are accepted.

Front Street and Cowboy Museum

This replicated old town area allows visitors to experience the Wild West. Ogallala was once the northernmost point on the cattle drives. The free museum displays artifacts from the area cowboys who traveled through town. Take home a piece of the West from the general store. During the summer, experience a Wild West show that includes an authentic shootout.

Petrified Wood Gallery

What can be done with petrified wood? If your name is Howard or Harvey Kenfield, plenty. These twin brothers have been designing with natural elements for over half a century. Their craft demands certain skills, and manipulating petrified wood requires specific cutting tools. Creating mosaic fragments out of pictures requires creativity.

Framed three-dimensional petrified wood structures line the gallery walls. Each detailed piece took about two months to make. Carved birds perch on sticks. Miniature structures have been turned into whimsical music boxes. A small carved cabin is paired with the song "Memories." "How Great Thou Art" is combined with one of the carved churches. Several carvings show the Kenfields' sense of humor. A crank ice cream bucket features "For the Good Times." The small carved outhouse structure plays "Alone Again Naturally."

In addition to the petrified wood carvings, polished stones and agates are also displayed. Through the years, the brothers went to rock shows to add to their collection and to find materials for their creations. Spheres were chipped out of stone and then polished. Collected arrowheads turned into framed art designs. The Kenfields' dedication to their craft is astounding.

Additional collections are on loan from other artisans. Donated pewter sculptures of western figures are organized behind glass. Each collection includes a framed article telling more about the donors. Western art is treated with care.

Although monetary donations are welcome, this museum is free for visitors. In the gift shop, some petrified wood carvings are for sale. My miniature carved cross will always be a treasured souvenir.

If you are lucky, one of the twins will be manning the studio the day you visit. I was doubly lucky, as both brothers came by the day of my visit. My short stop turned into a satisfying longer one. Getting to see the art through the eyes of the creators was amazing. This stop will forever be one of my favorite Nebraska destinations.

Lake McConaughy Water Interpretive Center

Water management is crucial in this part of the state. Drought cycles continued to show the need to create an irrigation source. In 1935, the Public Works Administration approved funding for a hydroelectric project in the area. Kingsley Dam began operations in 1941, and the reservoir, Lake McConaughy, was one result.

At the visitor's center south of the dam, learn more about this important water source. Underneath the ground, the High Plains Aquifer helped to make the irrigation project possible. Managing this limited resource is paramount. The Platte River also needs protection.

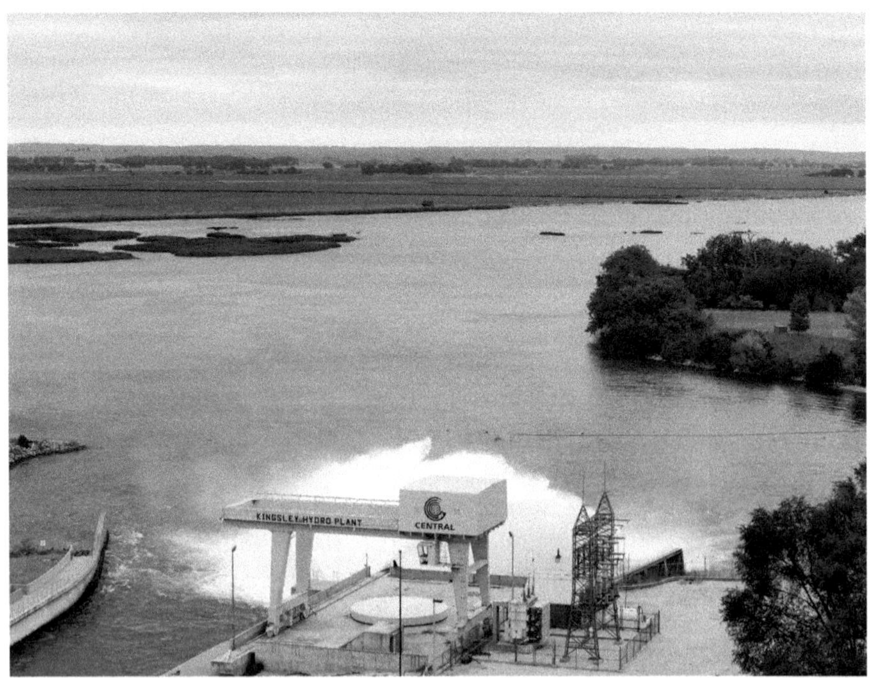

As the world's second-largest hydraulic fill dam, Kingsley Dam affects both Lake McConaughy and Lake Ogallala.

Besides telling about water management, the museum encourages visitors to go deeper. At the start, visitors are greeted with a rare Nebraska diving bell, once used to go far beneath the lake's surface to check for debris. With lift-the-flap displays throughout, interactive learning is encouraged. "Water in Motion" shows the changes in the Platte River through time-lapse video. Through film clips, visitors can observe the dam construction firsthand. A light-up display shows the impact of water sources. Exhibits demonstrate hydroelectricity. Kids can even "catch" a fish and learn a bit about water safety.

7

PANHANDLE

The western edge of Nebraska is distinctive. Known as the Nebraska Panhandle, this part of the state has a different time zone and area code. More than that, this area is known for its dramatic geographical features.

Lewellen Locations

With its sweet water spring, the Ash Hollow area was a popular Overland Trail Route stop. The surrounding hills were challenging for early travelers. But this valley section provided respite, and a large hillside cave offered shelter. Archaeological evidence suggests that both Native Americans and early white settlers used this location. Today, visitors to Ash Hollow State Park can still see this cave through a clear barricade.

To learn more about the first people who traveled through this area, a stop at the visitor's center is recommended. Displays tell the tales of battles and fossil finds. Artifacts authenticate the experiences. The stories are fascinating, and community volunteers keep this museum going.

Hiking the hills at this park is highly suggested. Since rattlesnakes are present in the area, sandals are not recommended. In the lower part of the park, travelers can peek into the windows of a rare stone schoolhouse. Bird-watching opportunities are also plentiful.

At the edge of the park is the Windlass Hill. At the bottom of the hill is a reconstructed sod house and a covered wagon bridge. While the path is paved to the top of this lofty hill, slow and steady hiking is suggested. The breathtaking panoramic views make the steep climb worth the effort. Near the crest of the hill, wagon ruts were embedded into the trails by long-ago lumbering oxen. An Oregon Trail marker tells about the prevalent pioneer presence.

On the way to the town of Lewellen is the Ash Hollow Cemetery. Here locals honor the grave of one pioneer. Traveling west in 1849, newlywed Rachel Pattison took ill one morning. By evening, she was dead from cholera. The original marker made by her grieving husband is now protected from the elements.

The Most Unlikely Place, a gallery, café and coffee shop in Lewellen, is a place to "lift the spirit and feed the soul." It is open Wednesday through Saturday from mid-March through mid-December. The art, consisting of oils, watercolors, pastels, sculpture and glass etching, is created by three siblings.

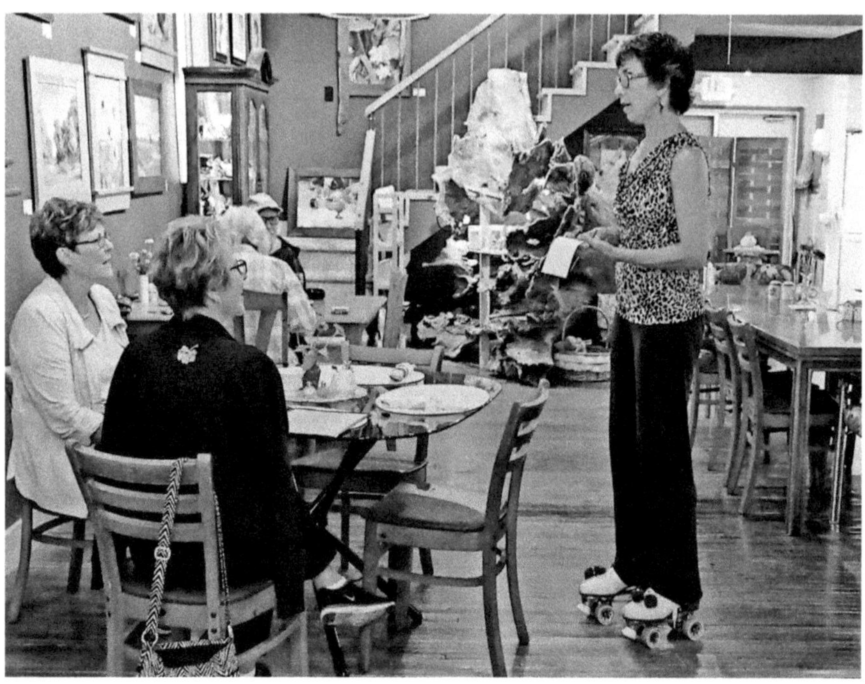

Cynthia Miller serves up food orders in a fun way at the Most Unlikely Place.

This delightful place serves breakfast and lunch and specializes in "healthy choice" options. Entrées feature local and natural ingredients, and the kitchen will cater to guests with special dietary needs. You may enter as a stranger, but you'll leave as a friend.

CHEYENNE COUNTY

In 1867, when Nebraska became a state, Sidney became a town. The fact that this location was named for a lawyer is rather ironic, as soon this location became known as the "Wickedest City in the West." Sidney Barracks were built to protect Union Pacific Railroad interests in this "Toughest Town on the Tracks."

The barracks were planned as a temporary outpost. Once the site needed to be more permanent, quarters were moved a block and renamed Fort Sidney. At one point, the fort had forty buildings. During the Indian Wars, a strong military presence was necessary. Fort Sidney soon became a significant traveler supply site.

During the Black Hills Gold Rush, many treasure seekers stopped to outfit their wagons. These men were often rougher, and outlaws were also drawn to Sidney. At one time, eighty saloons and gambling rooms were in this small community. Nightlife seekers had many options, including the world's first twenty-four-hour theater.

Proximity to the railroad and cattle trails did help Fort Sidney thrive for a time. Supplying freighters and stagecoaches kept the townfolk busy. Once the railroads changed travel routes, the gold rush crowd shifted. In 1894, the fort closed. Five years later, the buildings were sold.

Today, visitors can tour three restored buildings. The former officers' quarters is now the Cheyenne County Museum. Tour the post commander's historically decorated home. The octagonal powder house can also be seen.

Throughout the year, Fort Sidney hosts various events. At Christmas, community organizations decorate certain rooms for the holidays. Lamplight tours also present area history. Near the fort is Boot Hill Cemetery. Both soldiers and Wild West victims are buried there.

In the thriving nearby town of Potter, experience bowling the old-fashioned way. Above the former hardware store, three unique lanes are waiting for strikers. This is the only duckpin bowling center west of the Mississippi.

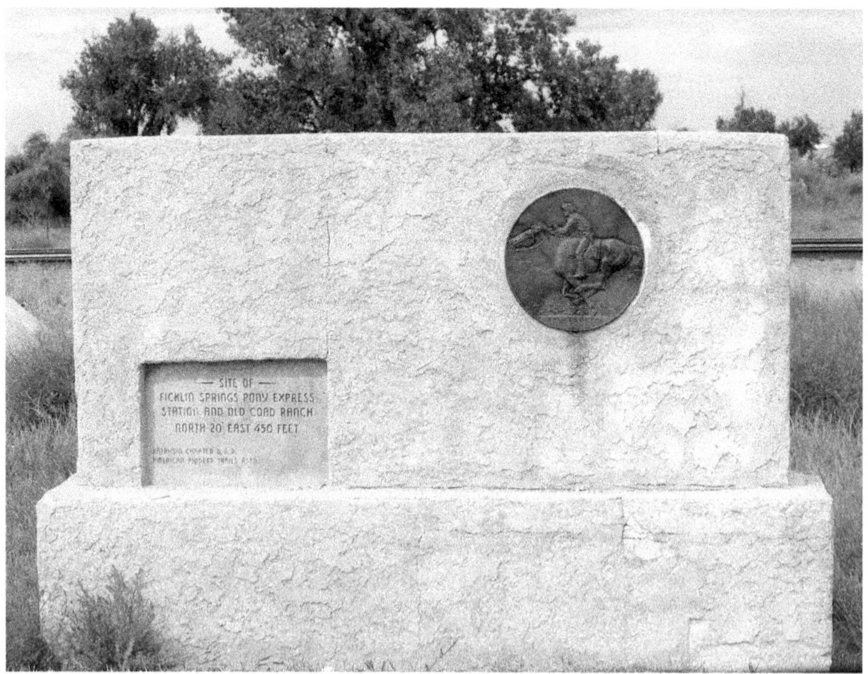

The Pony Express traveled 441 miles across Nebraska. This is one marker that visitors can see in the Panhandle.

Played with smaller six-inch balls, the pins used are rubber-headed and more rotund. Without automation, people are directly involved in the process; pin setters sit atop a ledge at the end of the lanes. For safety's sake, careful throws are recommended. Open by appointment, three lanes of interactive bowling are available.

After completing frames, stop by the nearby Potter Sundry for its specialty, tin roof sundaes. Or stop at Bags for a cool drink. Potter also has two museums. The Potter Depot Museum is on Front Street, and the Potter Historical Museum is located on Sherman Street.

Kimball County

Near Kimball and Bushnell is the Tri-State Monument. Nebraska, Wyoming and Colorado all meet at this point. In the 1860s, Congress had set the state boundaries, but astronomer and surveyor Oliver N. Chaffee disagreed with its measurements. The 41st parallel latitude and 27th degree latitude intersected at this locale. On August 17, 1869, he marked that spot as the intersection instead. Despite the fact that Congress's lines were several hundred feet away, Chaffee's measurements stuck. Today, a black fence guards the original marker. To get to this site, traveling private roads is necessary. Please be respectful of property boundaries.

At 5,424 feet, nearby Panaroma Point is the highest spot in Nebraska and provides quite the view. On a clear day, the observant can even see the Rocky Mountains. Although this is now private property, visitors can make the trip to the promontory for a small admission fee. This is range land. If buffalo are nearby, do not seek them out for an up-close photo opportunity. These lumbering animals can be rather dangerous. To mark the momentous occasion of hiking to the top of Nebraska, a celebration is in order. Visitors can stop by the Kimball-Banner County Chamber of Commerce offices for a climbing certificate. If you visit after hours, e-mail your address and climbing date. The chamber is willing to mail out certificates.

SCOTTSBLUFF COUNTY

Scottsbluff's Riverside Discovery Center is a zoo with a park attached. This location is home to 130 native and exotic animals—14 of them are endangered. With kids in mind, new exhibits have been created. The Dino Dig is an interactive experience. During the hot summers, kids can cool off in the splash pad. On site is also a petting zoo for all to get a firsthand experience with the animals.

Two locations in Gering were telling about local history. At the Farm and Ranch Museum, agriculture was the focus. The North Platte Valley Historical Museum emphasized town history. In 2013, these museums combined to form the Legacy of the Plains. Now they are preserving the past with a single-minded focus.

With a recent expansion, the museum now can show more of its collections. For years, community members had dropped off items. Due to lack of space, piles were random and unlabeled. Now, artifacts are unpacked and displayed. Wardrobes show clothes from one era. Local businesses, including Terrible Terry's Fuel Center, are emphasized. Exhibits show differences between irrigated and dry land farming. Displays show the differences between ranching and farming. Travel and transport exhibits cover trails and trains. Although

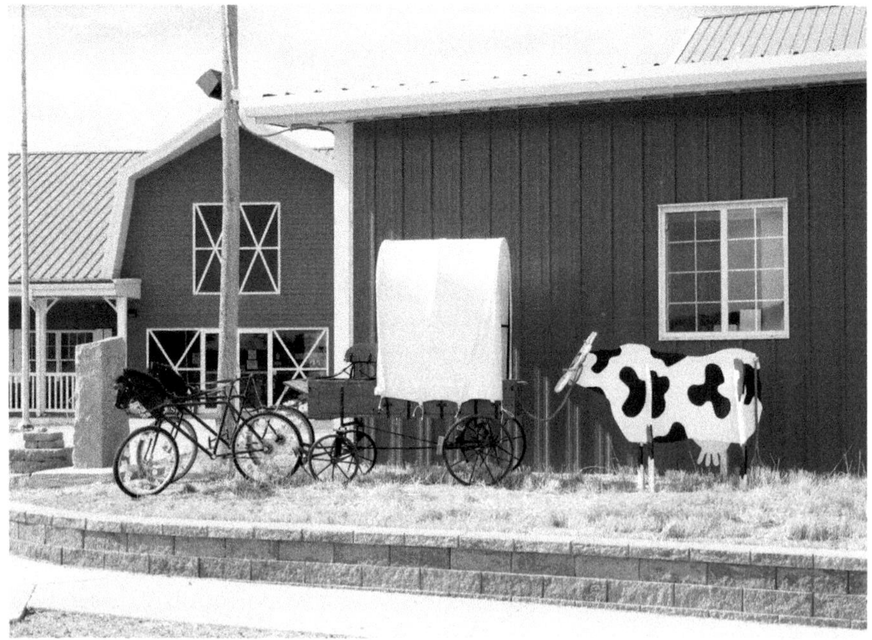

Visitors enjoy this whimsical entrance to the Legacy of the Plains Museum.

most displays are permanent, some artifacts do rotate. Temporary exhibits feature different themes, such as the tumbleweed.

Outdoors, a working farm surrounds the museum's buildings. Longhorn cattle graze on the grounds. When called by name, the cattle will meander up to be fed. Tractors plow the nearby fields, readying the museum's dedicated eighty acres for crops. On site is a blacksmith shop that demonstrates the art of making tools. Soon a sod house will be reconstructed at this location.

The Legacy of the Plains is always looking for ways to connect with the community. During "Puzzles of the Past" events, community members gather to identify people in long-ago photographs. Area residents share their own histories. At handcraft events, visitors can learn heritage skills such as rug hooking.

Other annual events provide visitors with more opportunities to connect with the past. The biggest event is the Harvest Festival. On this occasion, guests can see antique farming demonstrations. Audience participation is encouraged. Each year, different crops rotate between the fields. Tractors go on parade, and horse-drawn carriages give rides. People even pick potatoes. For a small fee per pound, produce goes home with visitors.

The Legacy of the Plains wants to reach out to a forgotten sector of the community. For the Lakota, the Scottsbluff Monument is very sacred. At one point, tribes held gatherings at the top. Now the Circle the Bluffs Pow Wow is bringing back that tradition. A permanent arbor is built on the grounds for their ceremonies. Thundering drums shake the ground. Echoing beats can again be heard for miles.

These prominent bluffs were named for early trapper Hiram Scott, who died while in the area. Between these bluffs is the notorious Mitchell Pass. This was one route often used by pioneers traveling west. The Scottsbluff National Monument now protects this important landmark.

At the onsite Oregon Trail Museum and Visitor's Center, this landmark's history is documented. The artwork and photographs of William Henry Jackson make the monument come alive. Travelers can still follow trails to the top. Talk to park rangers to determine the best hiking routes for your group.

Several miles away is the former site of Fort Robidoux Trading Post. Mentioned in many diaries, this post provided needed supplies. The local

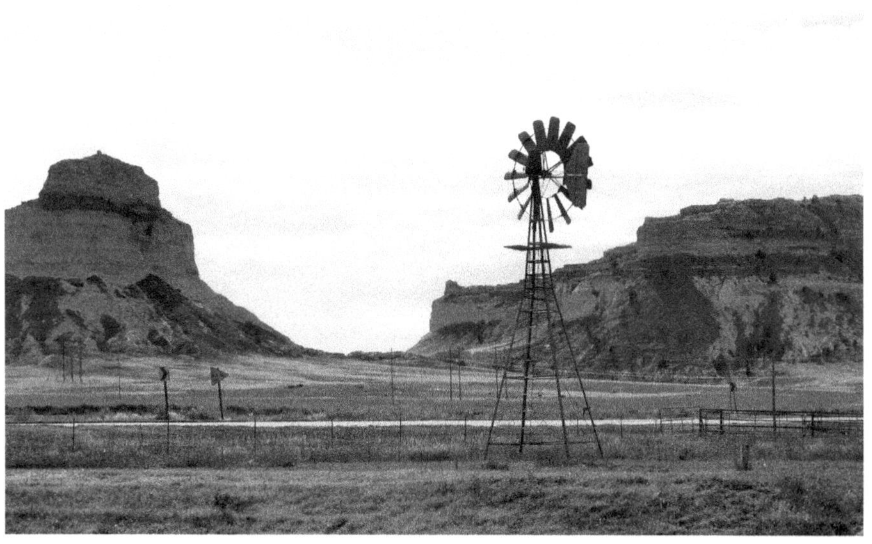

In western Nebraska, windmills are needed for survival.

blacksmith had made repairs and put new shoes on horses. Wagon ruts and markers show where history was made. Despite being an easier pioneer crossing, this site was later abandoned. Mitchell Pass was more direct. In Carter Canyon is a life-size reconstruction of that early post. Visitors take self-guided tours.

Nearby is Lake Minatare. In 1916, this lake formed during the Pathfinder Irrigation Project. Initially, this was one of four North Platte Wildlife Refuge sites. Used for irrigation and animal habitat protection, this reservoir is still significant. Because it is now a popular state recreation area, the official wildlife refuge status is no more. Yet every year during the fall and winter, the park closes to the public and becomes a migratory bird sanctuary.

Lake Minatare is also home to one of seven inland lighthouses found across the country. Built by jobless veterans during the Great Depression, the lighthouse stands fifty-five feet tall. Constructed from native stone, the Minatare Lighthouse stands strong. Visitors can enjoy unobstructed views of the area from the observation tower.

Morrill County

Nearby the natural formations of Jail House and Courthouse Rocks is the community of Bridgeport. Here visitors can tour the Pioneer Trails Museum. Presenting local history is the mission of this small-town museum. Several miles outside of town is the Chimney Rock Monument. When approaching, one cannot help but think of all the pioneers who came before. This landmark rock signified progress on their long journey west.

Over time, erosion and human destruction have altered the height of the monument. Yet this monument is still worth visiting. The excellent visitor's center only charges admission for adults. Interactive displays bring the past to life.

Box Butte County

The city of Alliance, officially founded in 1888, is "building the best hometown in America." When the land was platted, there was a hostile takeover. Alliance swallowed up the nearby town of Grand Lake. The

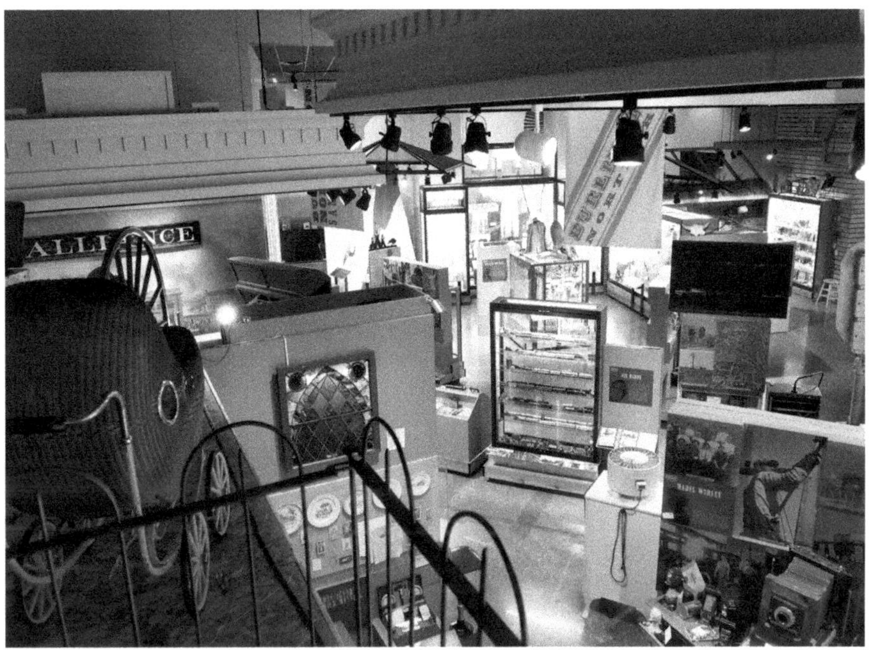

Alliance's Knight Museum and Sandhill Center brings local history to life.

Lincoln Land Company bought railroad land, and new settlers snatched up all the area property. Growth was swift.

Keeping early schools open was a challenge. Eastern schoolteachers seemed to marry off right away. After this kept happening, the town advertised for homely women. This did not work either. But the restrictive clause forcing teachers to stay single for two years did help.

When fires gutted three early buildings, the volunteer fire department formed. The Nebraska Stockgrowers Association started to assist farmers and ranchers. Many moved to the area because of the railroad. Alliance soon had two distinctions. Due to being the proclaimed "Potato Center of Nebraska," the school newspaper is still the *Spud*. As the "Cattle Capital of Nebraska," residents operated the second-largest sale barn west of Omaha for a season.

After the initial population rush, Alliance's growth was steady. Today, the town is thriving. Its proximity to the Black Hills and Denver makes this a popular place to visit. Due to city support, admission is free to all area attractions. These museums tell the stories of the community's past and present future possibilities.

Recently remodeled, the Knight Museum of the Sandhills now features Smithsonian-style exhibits. Five themes are presented in the excellent portrayal of local history. Both "Life in the Sandhills" and "Town and Country" show the challenges of pioneering days. "Native American Life" tells about the first people to live in the area. Showing the personal side of early Alliance citizens is "The Rogues, Rascals and Visionaries" section. "The Railroad" truly did tie all citizens together. Woven together, these five stories capture the essence of the Alliance area.

What is especially noteworthy at the Knight Museum is the quality research area. Genealogists come from around the world to learn more about family history. Many of their records are starting to be available online.

Dobby's Frontier Town started when the visionary founder wanted to preserve western Nebraska history. Kenneth Dobby Lee saved nineteen historical buildings from destruction. Now volunteers keep his legacy alive with live reenactments in this reconstructed town. To make history more accessible, many of the buildings have interactive displays. The operators trust visitors will see the value of the exhibits and take care as they explore. This pretend town settlement brings the actual past into a whole new light.

The Sallows Military Museum's stated purpose is to "remember, honor and educate." Displays show various kinds of military memorabilia, most of which has been donated by local residents. This means that war is represented from the area's point of view. All American military conflicts from the past century have their own displays.

At the museum is a large area commemorating the former Alliance air base. Home to the 507th Paratroopers and Glider Pilots during World War II, this base was busy. The added soldiers caused the town population to double during that time. Now that site is the Nebraska State Veterans Cemetery.

CARHENGE

For a season, Nebraskan Jim Reinders called England home. Already an artist at heart, he became fascinated with Stonehenge. He visited often and became quite familiar with its design.

In 1982, Reinders's father died. When the family gathered to console one another, they decided to memorialize him. This family evidently likes grand gestures, because a Stonehenge replica was discussed. They agreed to meet in five years to carry out the vision.

Exactly how the thirty-nine vintage American automobiles were collected is unclear. In preparation, all were painted gray. Thirty-five Reinders family members gathered that day in June 1987 to carry out the plans. Pits dug five feet deep hold some of the cars trunk down. Welding the bridge sections was another task. The heel stone is a 1962 Caddy. During the 1987 summer solstice, the family celebrated the completed Carhenge with champagne, poetry, songs and even an original play.

Over time, more art has been added. Inspired by Vivaldi's symphony, Reinders's *Ford Seasons* showcases Nebraska's seasonal landscape changes. The Car Art Reserve is on the nearby hill. Artist Geoff Sandhurst won a contest with his car sculpture of a spawning salmon. Besides earning a cash prize, his art can be seen on the Carhenge grounds.

SHERIDAN COUNTY

The small town of Gordon celebrates its heritage at two locations. Near Wayland Park is the Scamahorn Museum, named after town founder Reverend John Scamahorn. Located in the original 1885 Methodist church, displays tell about early town history, including the trade territory that affected early merchants. Across town at Winship Park is the Tri State Oldtime Cowboy's Memorial Museum. For almost fifty years, this museum has honored those who served as ranch hands and rodeo cowboys. Exhibits include authentic western ranching relics. During the annual Willow Tree Festival, the town remembers the importance of continuing to meet and work together.

DAWES COUNTY

Chadron State College Museums

In 1938, geology professor Eleanor Barbour Cook began to seek out specimens for study. As her father was a famous paleontologist, she had contacts worldwide. Cook formed the Eleanor Barbour Cook Museum of Geology to display her natural history finds. The collection contained fossils, minerals, shells, mounted birds and mounted mammals. Her assistant, Albert Potter, and many others contributed specimens.

Within a decade, both Cook and Potter had moved on. Without supervision, many collected items were lost or stolen. Hardly any were recovered. In recent years, Chadron State College science professors have been developing this museum again. More vertebrate fossils have been introduced. Additional minerals and rocks help the museum to reflect the geology aspect of the museum. Contact the museum coordinator to arrange a visit or to learn more about the collection.

Educating students in astronomy is the mission of the Chadron State College Planetarium. Throughout the school year, public presentations teach stargazers to recognize constellations. School programs are available for public, private and homeschool students. Recently, the site introduced a Boy Scout program. Night sky viewing will help local Scouts earn badges and pins. Star parties utilize the science department's telescopes for outdoor viewing. Donations are encouraged, and fees are charged for certain events.

The High Plains Herbarium features medicinal plants and historic pharmaceuticals. Used as a teaching tool, the collection has been expanded greatly over the past five decades. Most of the sixty thousand varieties of vegetation are from the Nebraska High Plains area. Area Native Americans led the way in homeopathic treatments. Specimens displayed include rarely seen plants such as globemallow, snake weed and scarlet bugler. Open hours follow the college schedule. During summertime, the staff's required field work may limit accessibility.

Western Author Mari Sandoz

Growing up in an immigrant home restricted Mari Sandoz from learning English. But limitations never seemed to stop Mari for long. Despite an incomplete childhood education, Sandoz went to college. She wanted to write. The hundreds of book rejection slips did not faze her either. Instead, she gained experience editing and writing for newspapers.

While on his deathbed, Mari's father asked her to tell his life story. Since her childhood was rather rough, this request surprised her. Persistence was again required, as every publishing house refused her manuscript. After years of trying, *Old Jules* became her first published book. Sandoz had to fight for the right to keep her distinctive slang in the manuscript.

Most of Sandoz's books are rather harsh and graphic about life on the plains. Sometimes her titles were banned from libraries. Gradually, many readers and critics began to appreciate her realistic portrayals. Her biography of *Crazy Horse* using Lakota terms will always be monumental. Mari Sandoz knew the High Plains. Her works reflected her life.

The Mari Sandoz High Plains Heritage Center in Chadron has exhibits on Sandoz's life. Literature is also emphasized, especially her own titles. Permanent exhibits reflect the history and culture of the area. The C.F. Coffee gallery promotes local cattle ranching history.

MUSEUM OF THE FUR TRADE

The first influential industry in the Nebraska region was the fur trade. Traders desired buffalo hides, and Native Americans wanted store-bought goods. An established system benefited both. At the site of an early trading post outside of Chadron, the Museum of the Fur Trade was established. Preserving the history of this long-ago business is the museum's mission.

Exhibits have been carefully constructed. Over time, the museum has amassed an extensive collection of original guns. These weapons were manufactured specifically for the Native Americans. One side of the main exhibit hall chronicles the fur trade timeline. The other side contains the history of objects used in the trading process. Many items commemorate the Lewis and Clark expedition and the original mountain men. The traded textiles were the most significant for the Native Americans. Only part of the museum's accumulated collection of authentic weavings is on display.

Outside, the plants grown in the Indian Garden are produced from ancient seeds. Over a century ago, pioneer horticulturist Oscar Will gathered native plants for preservation purposes. To maintain this stock, the plantings vary every year.

During the reconstruction of the trading post buildings, two locals were consultants. As children, they had visited the actual post. Their recollections added authenticity to the project.

The warehouse would have been filled from floor to ceiling with goods. An authentic robe press demonstrates how furs were processed. To help with shipping and storage, traded furs were baled into bundles of ten. Without this process, trading could not have happened.

Highlighting the outdoor exhibits is the restored 1837 original trading post. Excavations helped determine the original footprint. Most trading posts had two rooms. Private family quarters would have been in the cramped back room while the front room was open to the public.

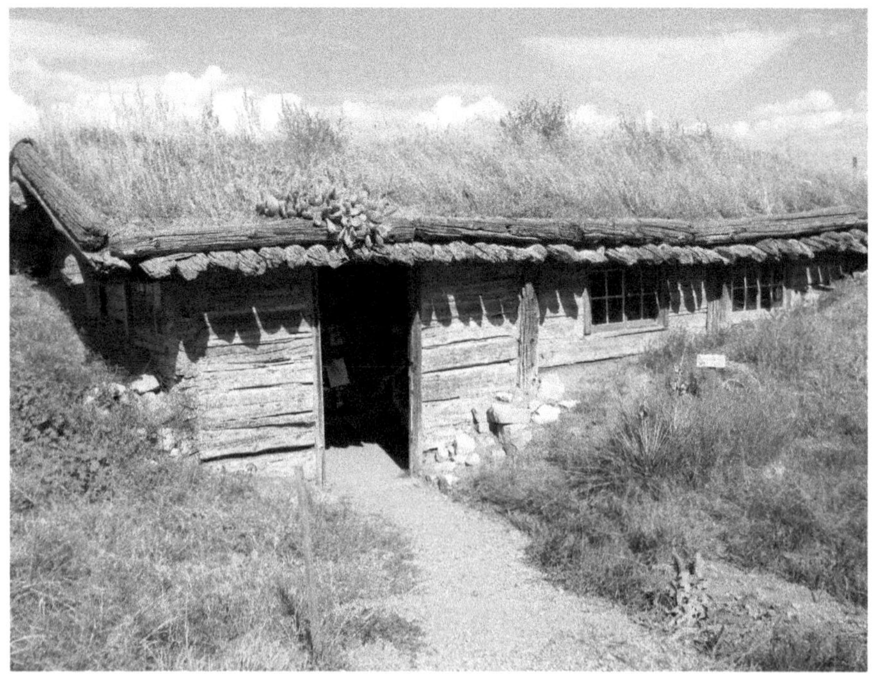

At the Fur Trade Museum, this small sod building was reconstructed on the original foundation of James Bordeaux's 1837 trading post.

Upon entering, potential traders would see shelves stocked with desired goods. Everything from combs to coffee to gunpowder kept the bartering system moving. Tomahawks, arrowheads and even beads were available for purchase. Unfortunately, to the Native Americans' detriment, whiskey was also a popular commodity. At the time, a flintlock gun cost five buffalo robes. A knife or five yards of cotton print required one robe for trade. Besides trading, the post served as a social hall and a place for gathering news.

Historical handwritten eyewitness accounts documented more details. The original post housed James "the Bear" Bordeaux and his wives, "High Red Woman" (Marie) and "Intestines Woman" (Annie). After he began trading at multiple locations, Bordeaux ultimately abandoned this post. Illegal arms dealer Francis Boucher stepped into this location. Fighting to keep Native Americans on their homelands was his desire. After the Battle of Little Big Horn in 1876, these natives were forced out. The post closed for good, and the buildings collapsed a few years later. Now at the Fur Trading Museum, the reconstructed post reflects these details.

FORT ROBINSON

From the start, Fort Robinson served many purposes. First, this location kept local citizens safe during the Indian Wars. Famed Sioux chief Crazy Horse died here, and a monument remembers his impact on the area. The Red Cloud Agency was also near the fort. For a time, a cavalry remount was stationed at Fort Robinson. Then the K-9 crew moved on site to train war dogs. During World War II, a large German POW camp provided prisoners to work area farms. When the army moved on, a beef research station used some buildings.

The Fort Robinson Learning Center and Landmark Store tells of this fort's history. Around the grounds, additional reconstructed buildings and barracks allow visitors to see the fort as it was. Before visiting, visitors may want to learn even more about the fort's past. Former resident historian Tom Buecker's book *Fort Robinson and the American West* tells more about the fort. For a fictional look, read Nebraska author Stephanie Grace Whitson's *Pine Ridge Portrait* series.

Today, Fort Robinson is a state park. Visitors can stay in the larger officers' quarters or in the former officers' row. During the summer, horseback riding, nature tours and other activities happen around the fort. This part of Nebraska is beautiful. Explore the area by taking a hike or a drive.

Also on site is the Trailside Museum of Natural History. Along Nebraska's "Fossil Freeway," the paleontology finds are plentiful. The most famous exhibit is "The Clash of the Mammoths." Evidently, long ago two mammals locked horns and then died that way. The fossils are intertwined forever. This museum features geological finds and has a great local rock collection.

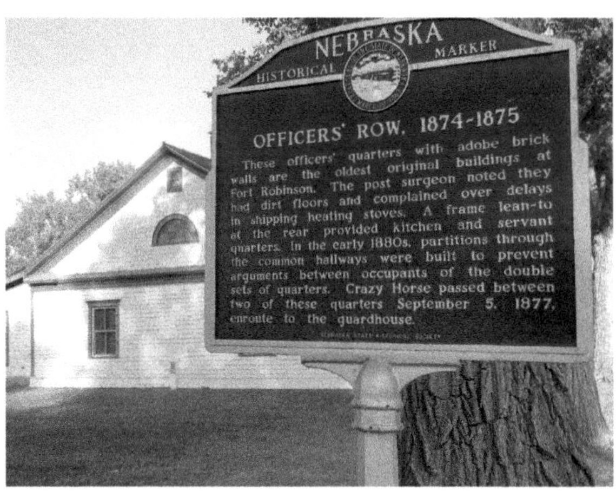

Travelers visiting Fort Robinson can stay on Officers' Row.

SIOUX COUNTY

Guadalcanal Memorial Prairie and Ranch

Almost five thousand acres encompass this Prairie Plains property found in northwest Nebraska. Donor Howard Juhl managed this land until 2005. Vista views, steep valleys, buttes and lowland meadows represent the classic high plains landscape. This property is diverse. Since this location is an active ranch, public access is only during Prairie Plains Resource Institute events. Please contact the institute to find out about any upcoming planned activities.

Off Highway 2

Sometimes dirt roads lead to the best destinations. Getting to the following places involves minimum-maintenance roads. Going on rainy days is not recommended, and access is limited at certain times. Originally, fur traders called this region, which extends into South Dakota, the Badlands. The miles of stark landscape seem desolate until you begin to explore.

High Plains Homestead

The town of High Plains seems to have been around for many decades. In reality, this western settlement is recently established. Abandoned buildings moved on site create authenticity, and reclaimed wood ages new construction. At the High Plains Homestead, owners Mike and Linda Kesselring provide guests with a quality rural experience.

So far, eight western-style buildings complete the homestead. The first two buildings are the typical locales that often service paying guests. At the Dirty Creek Saloon, thirsty travelers can still indulge either in alcohol or an ice-cold sarsaparilla. The Badlands Mercantile features antiques, both rare and commonplace. Many items are for sale.

The remaining buildings turn the homestead into a museum. In the early 1900s, the Deep Creek School educated some Sioux County residents. Guests can sit in period desks and and try to recall the facts featured on the walls. While children enjoy playing school, they might enjoy the next building even more. The High Plains Sheriff Office and

Jail delivers justice. Enjoy locking your fellow travelers up in the clink. Including limited outhouse usage for prisoners, the posted rules are rather amusing.

Four other small buildings also display history. The small homestead house shows how every bit of usable space held functional items. Pioneer life was nothing if not practical. Horses and a tractor are housed in the livery. Crammed with implements, the blacksmith and earthworks shop holds historic tools. Even the post office still has boxes just waiting for mail.

The Cookshack is considered the heart of the homestead. Guests can order "three squares a day" during spring, summer and fall. Hearty meals served cowboy style fill visiting cowpokes at a reasonable price. Coffee costs an advertised four bits, and baking is done on site. Diners should make reservations.

The bunkhouse consists of six western-themed rooms. Expected modern conveniences include air conditioning, bathrooms and an above-ground pool. Best yet, a substantial breakfast is included. Lacking are televisions and telephones. Wi-fi provides the only communication option. This location is more than just a place to bunk or find grub.

Until recently, this location completely shut down for the winter. Now the Sand Creek Cabin is open year round. To use this larger space, a three-day minimum stay is required. From December to April, the Cookshack closes. Guests must bring their own food and supplies.

Hudson-Meng Education and Research Center

Back in 1954, the USDA was working on a soil conservation dam project. One part involved blocking in a natural spring to form a stock pond. While digging, workers discovered some bones and assumed they were sheep bones. Construction continued. Area rancher Albert Meng and his friend, amateur archaeologist Bill Hudson, disagreed with the conclusions. From experience, they knew the bones were too large to be from sheep. The two men sought out a scientist's opinion. In 1968, Dr. Larry Agenbroad determined these bones were bison bones.

In 1971, this Chadron State College professor started an official onsite dig. Within a short time, he recognized the ground held a massive grave site. Scientists estimated that up to six hundred bison skeletons might be underground. Scientists at the Hudson-Meng Education and Research Center continue to research the site.

In 1997, builders constructed a climate-controlled building to cover the bison finds. Now visitors can observe the dig in action. A life-size bison sketch shows the large size of these lumbering plains creatures. Viewing the skeletal diagram helps observers to identify the buffalo parts.

Toadstool Geologic Park

Looking more like the moon than Nebraska, Toadstool Geologic Park is a hiker's paradise. Resembling mushrooms, the natural sculptures were fancifully called toadstools. Certain slabs of sandstone seem to hover in mid-air. This rocky area is a part of the Oglala National Grassland, and the U.S. Forest Service maintains this complex natural wonder.

Clay deposits, left behind by flooding, turned into stone over time, and volcanic ash drifted over from neighboring states. These materials combined to become the unique landscape still seen today. The observant eye can see fossilized tracks in the dry river bed created by wandering animals.

A reconstructed sod house sits near the central parking lot. Picnic tables provide space to absorb the unconventional landscape. Everyone can enjoy this park even if visitors are unable or unwilling to hike the sometimes steep trails. This location is open year round. Visitors need to pay a small fee for day use or to stay overnight in one of the six undeveloped camping sites.

All visitors can do their part to protect this geological wonder. Forging new paths should not result in the rock's destruction. Do not climb any unstable formations. Study the fossil and rock collecting guidelines before taking home any restricted souvenirs. Preserve this fascinating location for the next generations.

Agate Fossil Beds National Monument in Harrison

At Agate Springs Ranch, where horses and cattle roamed, another animal type was found—the fossilized kind. Like his ancestor who discovered Australia, rancher James Cook liked exploration. Wandering around his ranch, Cook noted natural phenomena, including fossils. To share his finds, he invited paleontologists to visit. These experts confirmed a burrowed bone bed was underneath his dirt. The Carnegie and University Hills bone bed, to be precise. This proved to be a globally significant find in the paleontology world. Eventually, Cook's son, Harold, would continue his father's fossil quest. He became an unofficial paleontologist as well.

Besides his fossil fascination, Cook became curious about Native American cultures and history. This started because of his friendship with Chief Red Cloud. As a young cattle herder, Cook stopped at the Red Cloud Agency on one of his drives. His quick thinking prevented a fight between his traveling companion and the Native Americans. Once the Indians were convinced the man was searching for bones and not gold, they welcomed him. At this point, Cook became an arbitrator as well.

Cook's friendship with Red Cloud lasted until the chief's death thirty-five years later. Red Cloud frequented the ranch and left tokens of appreciation. Often designed specifically for the Cooks, the gifts were priceless. Red Cloud gave them key Lakota cultural items as well. Today, the James Cook Collection Gallery houses these artifacts at the Agate Fossil Beds National Monument.

Two indoor rooms hold exhibits. Besides the Native American artifacts, a diorama showcases area fossil finds. Replicas of rare dinosaurs are re-created in bone bed fashion. Both actual and replica fossils are on display. A short video orients visitors to the location.

Three historic trails await hikers. The Daemonelix one-mile trail features ancient sand dunes and fossil grasslands. Observant eyes can see evidence of beavers' spiraled burrows. Below the overlook area is the original ranch spread. The immensity of the tablelands is evident.

Where James Cook found the fossils is now accessible to the public. The Fossil Hills 2.7-mile paved trail is even open to wheelchairs. Crossing over the Niobrara River and wetlands, the path loops through the University and Carnegie Hills. Along this path, explorers can learn the names of area plants and animals.

About midpoint, a side trail breaks off. This path leads to Harold Cook's 1910 restored cabin. Later on, this location was used by scientists who were excavating the fossil finds.

This remote national park has a junior ranger program where children learn to speculate like scientists. Students answer questions about the indoor displays. Then they explore outdoor surroundings. Successful completion of the challenges results in junior ranger certificates.

We have now covered many of Nebraska's 77,421 square miles. Whether you lean toward exploring Nebraska's historic destinations or natural wonders (or both types of adventures), my hope is that you will continue to enjoy the journey. This middle state has so much to offer. Detouring through Nebraska results in many wonderful experiences.

APPENDIX A

NEBRASKA HISTORICAL MUSEUMS AND SOCIETIES

Exploring local Nebraska museums is the best way to learn about Nebraska. Generally, these treasure-troves of history are staffed by local volunteers. These men and women are truly vested in preserving their communities' histories. Listed below are all Nebraska county historical societies. Any organizations without actual museums are noted with an asterisk.

Metro Region

Cass County Historical Society Museum in Plattsmouth
Dodge County Historical Society, May Museum in Fremont
Douglas County Historical Society, General Crook House in Omaha
*Lincoln-Lancaster County Genealogical Society
Sarpy County Historical Museum in Bellevue
Saunders County Historical Museum in Wahoo
Washington County Historical Museum and Frahm House in Fort Calhoun

Pioneer Region

Butler County Museum in David City
Clay County Historical Society and Museum in Clay Center
Fillmore County Museum in Fairmont
Gage County Historical Society and Museum in Beatrice
Hamilton County Historical Society, Plainsman Museum in Aurora
Jefferson County Historical Society, Fairbury Museum in Fairbury
Nuckolls County Museum in Superior
Otoe County Museum of Memories in Syracuse
Polk County Historical Museum in Osceola
Richardson County Museum in Falls City
Saline County Historical Society and Museum in Dorchester
Seward County Historical Society Museum in Goehner
Thayer County Museum in Belvidere
York County Historical Society, Anna Palmer Museum in York

Lewis and Clark Region

Antelope County Historical Society and Museum in Neligh
Boone County Historical Museum in Albion
Cedar County Historical Museum in Hartington
Colfax County, Schuyler Museum/Colfax County Museum and Genealogy Society in Schuyler
Cuming County Historical Society and Museum Complex in West Point
Dakota County Historical Society and O'Connor House Museum in Dakota City
Dixon County Historical Society and Museum in Allen
Madison County Historical Society Museum in Madison
Merrick County Historical Society Museum in Central City
Nance County Historical Society Museum, Fullerton Museum in Fullerton
Pierce County Historical Society and the Pierce Museum in Pierce
Platte County Historical Society Museum in Columbus
Stanton County Heritage Museum in Stanton
Wayne County Historical Museum in Wayne

Sandhills Region

Arthur County Historical Society and Courthouse Museum in Arthur
Blaine County Historical Society in Brewster
*Boyd County Historical and Genealogical Societies
Brown County Historical Society and Coleman House Museum in Ainsworth
Cherry County Historical Society and Museum in Valentine
Custer County Historical Society and Museum in Broken Bow
Garfield County Historical Society Museum in Burwell
Grant County Historical Society and Grant County Courthouse in Hyannis
Greeley County Historical Society Courthouse Museum in Greeley
Holt County Historical Society Museum in O'Neill
Hooker County Historical Society and Museum in Mullen
Howard County Historical Society and Historical Village in St. Paul
Keya Paha County Historical Society and Museum in Springview
*Logan County Historical Society
Loup County Historical Society, Sunnyside School District Museum in Taylor
McPherson County Historical Society, display at the Tryon courthouse
Rock County Historical Museum in Bassett
Sherman County Historical Society and Museum in Loup City
Thomas County Historical Museum in Thedford
Valley County Historical Society and Museum in Ord
Wheeler County Historical Society Courthouse Museum in Bartlett

Frontier Trails Region

Adams County Historical Society, Hastings Museum in Hastings
Buffalo County Historical Society, Trails and Rails Museum in Kearney
Dawson County Museum in Lexington
Franklin County Museum in Franklin
Furnas-Gosper Historical Society and Museum in Arapahoe
Hall County Historical Society, Stuhr Museum in Grand Island
Harlan County Historical Museum in Orleans
Kearney County Historical Museum in Minden
Phelps County Historical Society, Nebraska Prairie Museum in Holdrege
Webster County Historical Museum in Red Cloud

PRAIRIE LAKES REGION

Chase County Historical Museum in Imperial
*Dundy County Historical Society
*Frontier County Historical Society
Hayes County Historical Society Museum in Hayes Center
Hitchcock County Historical Society and Museum Complex in Trenton
Keith County Historical Society, Mansion on the Hill in Ogallala
*Perkins Historical Society
Red Willow County, High Plains Historical Society and Museum in McCook

PANHANDLE REGION

Banner County Historical Society in Harrisburg
Box Butte County Historical and Genealogical Society, Knight Museum and Sandhills Center in Alliance
Cheyenne County Historical Association, Fort Sidney Museum in Sidney
Dawes County Historical Society and Museum in Chadron
Deuel County Historical Society, Union Pacific Depot Museum in Chappell
Historical Society of Garden County, Silver Hill Museum in Oshkosh
Kimball County, Plains Historical Museum in Kimball
Morrill County Historical Society, Pioneer Trails Museum in Bridgeport
Scotts Bluff County, Represented by Legacy of the Plains in Gering
Sheridan County Historical Society, Armstrong House Museum in Rushville
Sioux County Historical Society and Museum in Harrison

Cultural Nebraska

From Native Americans to immigrants, Nebraska represents the melting pot concept. Across the state, learn more about these varied cultures by visiting these locations.

Metro Region

Blair: Danish American Archive and Library

Lincoln: American Historical Society of Germans from Russia, Asian Community and Cultural Center

Omaha: Czech and Slovak Educational Center and Cultural Museum; El Museo Latino: The first Latino Art, History and Cultural Center in the Midwest; Great Plains Black History Museum; Nebraska Jewish Historical Society: Henry and Dorothy Riekes Museum

Pioneer Region

Henderson Mennonite Heritage Park

Strombsurg: Swedish Midsommer Festival

Syracuse: Germanfest and Tannebaum festivities

Wilber Czech Museum

Wymore: Great Plains Welsh Heritage Centre

Lewis and Clark Region

Niobrara: Ponca Tribal Museum

Oakland: Swedish Heritage Center

O'Neill: Nebraska's Irish Capital, celebrations around St. Patrick's Day

Sandhills

Dannebrog: Danish Capital of Nebraska

Dannebrog: Pawnee Arts Center

Panhandle

Ashton: Polish Heritage Center

CHILDREN'S MUSEUMS

Across the state, five children's museums cater to the younger crowd. For forty years, the Omaha Children's Museum has served up fun for all ages. Regional habitats are part of the water exhibit, and other displays let kids play grownup. The ball area teaches unsuspecting children scientific principles. Art is emphasized. Upstairs, the rotating exhibits are popular and provide more experiences.

At the Lincoln Children's Museum, crowd favorites include the prairie dog tunnels, water zone and theatrical stage. Bricks tumble down from the Cuckoo Construction three-story clock tower. Grow Zone allows the youngest ones to explore. Sponsored by specific local businesses, Tiny Town encourages kids to imagine life as a farmer, mechanic or more. Planes, trains and rocket ships make up the top floor.

Out in central Nebraska, three smaller museums entertain: the North Platte Museum, the Kearney Children's Museum and the Children's Museum of Central Nebraska in Hastings. The motto of the Children's Museum of Central Nebraska sums up the value of these interactive locations: "Where Children Play to Learn, and Grown-ups Learn to Play!"

Visit Nebraskamuseums.org for even more locations worth exploring.

APPENDIX B

ART ACROSS NEBRASKA

Past Nebraska Artwork

During the 1930s and '40s, artists were commissioned by the Treasury Department's Section of the Fine Arts. Through murals, painters captured the spirit of Nebraska. Post office buildings contain these artworks.

Pioneer Region

Auburn: *Threshing* by Ethel Magafan (1938)
Geneva: *Building a Sod House* by Edward Chavez (1941)
Hebron: *Stampeding Buffaloes Stopping the Train* by Eldora Lorenzini (1939)
Pawnee City: *The Auction* by Kenneth Evett (1942)

Lewis and Clark Region

Albion: *Winter in Nebraska* by Jenne Magafan (1939)
Schuyler: *Wild Horses by Moonlight* by Philip von Saltza (1940)

Sandhills Region

O'Neil: *Bailing Hay in Holt County in the Early Days* by Eugene Trentham (1938)
Valentine: *End of the Line* by Kady Faulkner (1939)

Frontier Region

Minden: *Military Post on the Overland Trail* by William E.L. Bunn (1939)
Red Cloud: *Loading Cattle, Stockade Builders* and *Moving Westward* by Archie Musick (1941)

Prairie Lakes Region

Ogallala: *Long Horns* by Frank Mechau (1938)

Panhandle Region

Crawford: *The Crossing* by G. Glenn Newell (1940)

PRESENT NEBRASKA ARTWORK

Two Nebraska artists are making their own marks across Nebraska today: Dave Reiser and Todd Williams.

Waverly artist Dave Reiser's murals are found at several Nebraska places mentioned in this book.

Columbus: Discovering the Colorful History of Columbus historical building mural
Grand Island: The Nebraska Building State Fair Outdoor Encounter Exhibits
Hastings Museum: The Kool-Aid Exhibit Mural
Kearney: Contributor at The Archway Monument
Odell: The one-hundred-foot transportation mural at the Old West Trails Center

Ogallala: Lake McConaughy's Water Interpretative Center
Omaha: The Henry Doorly Zoo

In 2012, Central City artist Todd Williams began his *Legacy of Nebraska* painting project. Over five years, Williams painted places from all ninety-three Nebraska counties. Featuring both historical and current locations, viewers will be visually transported into Nebraska. This project is now a part of the Nebraska sesquicentennial celebration. Throughout 2017, his 123 series paintings have traveled to certain locations across the state. In honor of 150 years of statehood, his art captures the spirt of Nebraska.

SOURCES

To feature so many Nebraska places involved extensive research. For almost every place mentioned in the book, I consulted websites and/or Facebook pages for reference between October 2016 and July 2017. I also had the privilege of communicating with many location experts via phone and e-mail. This lengthier list of websites and sources is available by request. Thanks to *Nebraska Life* and *NEBRASKAland* magazines for inspiration.

General

Perkey, Elton A. *Perkey's Nebraska Place Names*. 4th ed. Lincoln, NE: J&L Lee Co., 2003.

Legends of America, www.legendsofamerica.com/ne-forts.html.

Nebraska Association of County Officials, Nebraska County Individual Websites, http://www.nacone.org.

Nebraska Educational Television, www.NETNebraska.org.

Nebraska Game and Parks Commission, www.outdoornebraska.gov.

Nebraska Game and Parks Foundation, www.nebraskagameandparksfoundation.org.

Nebraska GenWeb project, http://www.rootsweb.ancestry.com/~negenweb.

Nebraska Museums, www.nebraskamuseums.org.

Nebraska State Historical Society, www.nebraskahistory.com.
Nebraska Tourism, www.visitnebraska.com.
NEGen Web Resource Project, usgennet.org/usa/ne/topic/resources.
NET's Nebraska Stories, www.NebraskaStories.org.
North American Forts, www.northamericanforts.com/West/ne.html.
Prairie Plains Resource Institute, prairieplains.org.
Virtual Nebraska, casde.unl.edu.
The Walking Tourists, www.thewalkingtourists.com.
West Nebraska, westnebraska.com.

METRO REGION

Guide to Exterior Art and Symbolism: Nebraska State Capitol. Lincoln, NE: Office of the Capitol Commission, 2006.
Guide to the Nebraska State Capitol. Norfolk: Nebraska Life Magazine, 2012.
Lukesh, Jean. *The Nebraska Adventure*. Layton, UT: Gibbs Smith, 2005.

Bess Streeter Aldrich, www.bessstreeteraldrich.org.
The Church of Jesus Christ of Latter-day Saints, https://www.lds.org/locations/mormon-trail-center-at-historic-winter-quarters.
Father Flanagan League, www.fatherflanagan.org.
Historic Florence, www.historicflorence.org.
Jun Kaneko, www.junkaneko.com.
Lincoln Firefighter's Museum, www.lincoln.ne.gov/city/fire/program/museum.
Lincoln Parks and Recreation, www.lincoln.ne.gov/city/parks/ParksFacilities/wetlands/wetlandsinfo.htm.
Lincoln's Ferguson House, www.environmentaltrust.org/about/ferguson.html.
Nebraska Capitol, www.capitol.nebraska.gov.
Nebraska Governor's Residence, www.governorsresidence.ne.gov.
Oh My! Omaha, www.ohmyomaha.com.
Omaha History, www.omahahistory.org.
Visit Omaha, www.visitomaha.com.
Weeping Water, www.weepingwaterhistory.com.

Pioneer Country

Brownville Historical Society, www.brownvillehistoricalsociety.org.
City of Seward, Nebraska, cityofsewardne.com.
Crete Heritage Society, www.creteheritage.org.
Hebron, Nebraska, hebronnebraska.us.
July Fourth Seward Nebraska, www.julyfourthseward.com.
Nebraska City Museum, www.gonebraskacity.com.
Nebraska Czechs of Wilber, www.nebraskaczechsofwilber.com.
Pawnee County, pawneecountynebraska.com.
Saline County History, salinehistory.org.
Saturday Evening Post, www.saturdayeveningpost.com.
Superior, Nebraska, cityofsuperior.org.

Lewis and Clark Region

American Memorials Directory, www.americanmemorialsdirectory.com/nebraska.html.
Exploring the Lewis and Clark Trail, lewisandclarkcountry.org.
Genoa Museum, megavision.net/genoamuseum.
Hochunk Inc. Winnebago Economic Development Corporation, hochunkinc.com.
Lewis and Clark Trail, lewisandclarktrail.com.
Winnebago Tribe of Nebraska, winnebagotribe.com.

Sandhills Region

Schweitzer, Amy. "Local St. Paul Firefighter Museum to Open During GCA Days." *Grand Island Independent*, July 7, 2010.

Nebraska Game and Parks Commission. "Smith Falls State Park." 6-15-2015 edition and a previous brochure.
Nebraska National Forests and Grasslands, https://www.fs.usda.gov/main/nebraska/home.

Nebraska Travels, www.nebraskatravels.com/tallest-waterfall-smith-falls-niobrara-river-ne.html.
Sandhills Journey Scenic Byway, sandhillsjourney.com.
St. Paul, Nebraska, stpaulnebraska.com.
Valentine, Nebraska, www.visitvalentine.org.

Frontier Trails

Arapahoe Pharmacy, arapahoepharmacy.com.
Cozad, Nebraska, cozadnebraska.net.
Furnas-GosperMuseum,www.arapahoe-ne.com/attractions/furnasgospermuseum.htm.
Robert Henri Biography, http://americanartgallery.org/artist/readmore/id/159.
Town of Gothenburg, gothenburgdelivers.com.
Virtual Cather, virtualcather.org.
Visit Kearney, www.visitkearney.org.
The Willa Cather Foundation, willacather.org.

Prairie Lakes

Discoe, Connie Jo. "Old Haigler School Becoming Museum." *McCook Gazette*, August 2, 2007.

Fort Cody, fortcody.com.
Kansas Travel blog, http://kansastravel.org/threecorners.htm.
Lake McConaughy, ilovelakemac.com.
Lincoln County, Nebraska, http://lincoln.negenealogy.org/fort_mcpherson.html.
Nebraskaland Days, nebraskalanddays.com.
North Platte Canteen, npcanteen.net.
Palisade Nebraska, palisadenebraska.com.
U.S. Department of Veterans Affairs, Fort McPherson National Cemetery, http://www.cem.va.gov/CEMs/nchp/ftmcpherson.asp.
Visit North Platte, visitnorthplatte.com.

PANHANDLE

Alliance, Nebraska, www.cityofalliance.net.
Chadron State College Museums, csc.com.
Dawes County, Nebraska, dawes-county.com.
Fossil Freeway Hudson Meng Bison Bonebed, fossilfreeway.net/hudson.php.
Kimball Area Tourism, visitkimball.com.
Kimball High Point of Nebraska, kimballne.org.
Legends of America Fort Robidoux, www.legendsofamerica.com/ne-plattevalleyoregontrail3.html.
Mari Sandoz Heritage Society, marisandoz.org.
Mari Sandoz High Plains Heritage Center, www.sandozcenter.com.
Nebraska Forests and Grasslands, https://www.fs.usda.gov/main/nebraska/home.
New Deal WPA Murals in Nebraska, wpamurals.org/nebraska.htm.
Potter, Nebraska, potterne.com.
Sidney Boothill Cemetery, www.sidneyboothill.com.
State Parks Fort Robinson State Park, www.stateparks.com/fort_robinson.html.
U.S. Fish and Wildlife Service North Platte National Wildlife Refuge, https://www.fws.gov/refuge/north_platte.

ABOUT THE AUTHOR

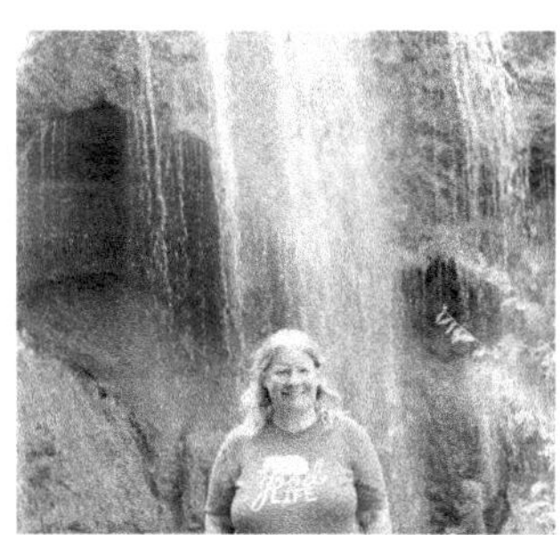

Gretchen (formerly Michels) Garrison and her family live in Lincoln, Nebraska. She helps her husband, Kyle, operate GP Restoration and Blasting. Besides homeschooling their four kids, Gretchen also curates the blog odysseythroughnebraska.com. Many of her articles have also been included in other Nebraska publications.

Visit us at
www.historypress.net

This title is also available as an e-book

www.ingramcontent.com/pod-product-compliance
Lightning Source LLC
LaVergne TN
LVHW052337100826
845147LV00020B/1092